SHORT TRIP TO THE EDGE

A Pilgrimage to Prayer

SCOTT CAIRNS

PARACLETE PRESS
BREWSTER, MASSACHUSETTS

2016 First Printing

Short Trip to the Edge: A Pilgrimage to Prayer

Copyright © 2016 by Scott Cairns

ISBN 978-1-61261-732-9

The Paraclete Press name and logo (dove on cross) are trademarks of Paraclete Press, Inc.

Library of Congress Cataloging-in-Publication Data

Names: Cairns, Scott.
Title: Short trip to the edge : a pilgrimage to prayer / by Scott Cairns.
Description: Brewster MA : Paraclete Press Inc., 2016.
Identifiers: LCCN 2015040570 | ISBN 9781612617329
Subjects: LCSH: Orthodox Eastern converts--United States--Biography.
Classification: LCC BX739.C35 A3 2016 | DDC 281.9092--dc23
LC record available at http://lccn.loc.gov/2015040570

10 9 8 7 6 5 4 3 2 1

Published by Paraclete Press
Brewster, Massachusetts
www.paracletepress.com

Printed in the United States of America

For Jackson Browne, whose songs during the '70s made me want to become a poet.

For Annie Dillard, my teacher, whose prose during the '70s showed me how to be one.

For Richard Howard, my friend, whose loving attention to the word I now recognize as true veneration.

CONTENTS

PREAMBLE

In spring of 2006, I first published *Short Trip to the Edge*, an account of my first three pilgrimages to *Agion Oros*, the Holy Mountain—a monastic peninsula in northern Greece that is perhaps more widely known as Mount Athos. It is, to be sure, a uniquely holy place, one of those places our Celtic saints would have characterized as *a thin place*. I understand their sense of such places as physical spaces in which the veil between heaven and earth seems transparent or porous, sites whose substance thins to yield apprehension of an occasion of greater substance; in my thinking, a more likely characterization of such scenes would be that they themselves have attained a palpable presence of the invisible enormity in which we live and move and have our being; that is, the places themselves register as *thick, full, densely inhabited by holy presence*.

Since those first three visits in 2004 and 2005, I have, at this writing, made an additional seventeen pilgrimages. Much has happened in the interim, and much more is afoot. Therefore, I had hoped for this edition to expand the epilogue of the original text in order to bring the reader a sense of an ongoing synergy, the collaboration between heaven and earth—which is what the Holy Mountain represents, and what the Holy Mountain performs. As it happens, the much more that is afoot is not quite ready for prime time; that is to say, we must be patient— which, among many other lessons from the fathers, is something I'm better at now than I was when I set out.

In the meantime, I have sought to correct what many have identified as an oversight; this edition includes both maps and photographs. This edition also does what I should have done from the first; with two exceptions—those of Father Iákovos and Father Matthew—I have changed the names of my beloved fathers in hopes of mitigating any undue attention to them, attention which might make more difficult the lives of prayer to which they are, by God's grace, committed.

Please accept this new edition as one that corrects certain errors of an enthusiastic pilgrim, and one that further extends the narrative to account for another several years along the way. *Good journey*, as the Greeks like to say—Καλό ταξίδι! *Good road*—Καλό δρόμο!

May your way be blessed.

Setting Out

In time, even the slowest pilgrim might
articulate a turn. Given time enough,

the slowest pilgrim—even he—might
register some small measure of belated

progress. The road was, more or less, less
compelling than the hut, but as the benefit

of time allowed the hut's distractions to attain
a vaguely musty scent, and all the novel

knickknacks to acquire a fine veneer of bone-
white dust, the road became then somewhat more

attractive; and as the weather made a timely
if quite brief concession, the pilgrim took this all

to be an open invitation to set out.

PART ONE

THE FAR

—— *Ouranoúpoli: Heaven's City* ——

—— *The Holy Mountain* ——

1

Lord, I believe. Help my unbelief.

The boat is the *Áxion Estín*, and I am finally on the boat.

The concrete pier at the bow marks the end of the world, where lies a modest village with an ambitious name; it is *Ouranoúpoli*, Heaven's City. We remain bound to its bustling pier by two lengths of rope as thick as my thigh.

Any moment now, the boat will be loosed and let go, and we will be on our way to *Agion Oros*, the Holy Mountain.

The air is sun-drenched, salt-scented, cool, and pulsing with a riot of gulls and terns dipping to grab bits of bread laid upon the water for them. The Aegean reflects the promising blue of a robin's egg. A light breeze dapples the surface, reflecting to some degree the tremor I'm feeling just now in my throat.

I've been planning this trip for most of a year.

I've been on this journey for most of my life.

For a good while now, the ache of my own poor progress along that journey has been escalating. It has reached the condition of a dull throb, just beneath the heart.

By which I mean, more or less, that *when I had traveled half of our life's way, I found myself stopped short, as within a dim forest.*

Or, how's this—*as I walked through that wilderness, I came upon a certain place, and laid me down to sleep: as I slept, I dreamed, and saw a man clothed with rags, standing with his face turned away from his own house, a book in his hand, and a great burden upon his back. He opened the book, and read therein; and, as he read, he wept and shook, and cried out, saying, What shall I do?*

Here's the rub: *by the mercy of God I am a Christian; by my deeds, a great sinner.*

You might recognize some of that language. You might even recognize the sentiment. These lines roughly paraphrase the opening words of three fairly famous pilgrims, the speakers of Dante's *Divine Comedy*, Bunyan's *The Pilgrim's Progress*, and the Russian devotional favorite known as *The Way of a Pilgrim*.

In each of them I find a trace of what Saint Paul writes to the church in Rome in the first century: *I do not understand what it is I do. For what I want to do, I do not do; but what I hate, I do.*

I get it. I really do get it.

In each of these confessions I suspect a common inference as well: something is amiss. There is a yawning gap between where I am and where I mean to go.

Lately, the crux of my matter has come pretty much down to this: having said prayers since childhood, I startled one day to the realization that—at the middling age of forty—I had not yet learned to pray.

At any rate, despite half a lifetime of mostly good intentions, I had not established anything that could rightly be called *a prayer life*.

I remember the moment of this realization with startling clarity, and with a good dose of chagrin. I was romping at the beach with Mona, our yellow Labrador. It was a gorgeous morning in early spring—absolutely clear, the air still crisp, tasting of salt from the bay, the water and sky mirroring a mutual, luminous turquoise.

I was throwing a stick of driftwood, repeatedly—as instructed in no uncertain terms by my ecstatic dog—into the Chesapeake for her to retrieve, and I was delighting in the sheer beauty of her astonishing leaps into the surf—wholehearted, jubilant, tireless—followed by her equally tireless insistence that I keep it up. She yelped, she pranced, she spun like a dervish as water poured from her thick coat into the flat sheen of sand at the water's edge.

In short, I was in a pretty good mood.

I was sporting cut-off jeans in February. I was barefoot. I was romping with my dog at the beach.

I was not the least bit depressed, nor even especially thoughtful. I had hardly a thought in my head at all.

I was, even so, feeling a good deal—feeling, actually, pretty pleased with myself, and feeling especially pleased with that radiant morning on the shore, accompanied by a deliriously happy dog. My best guess is that, after some years of high anxiety, I was finally relaxed enough to suspect the trouble I was in.

We had moved to Virginia Beach about a year earlier, having arrived there with a palpable sense of reprieve from a stint of—as I have come to speak of it—having *done time in Texas*. I had left a difficult and pretty much thankless teaching-and-program-directing job in north Texas in favor of a similar but far more satisfying gig at Old Dominion University in Norfolk. We'd extricated our little family—by which I mean me, Marcia, our ten-year-old Liz, and our five-year-old Ben—from our rundown cottage in a rundown corner of a small (and, at the time, relatively rundown) north Texas town; we'd swapped those derelict digs for a bright, airy bungalow by the beach.

The contrast was stunning. Our first evening there, in fact, sitting at an oceanfront café, we were treated to the spectacle of a dozen or more dolphins frolicking northward as they proceeded to the mouth of the Chesapeake half a mile up.

Life looked good. It looked *very* good. It even *tasted* good.

I felt as if I had found my body again after having misplaced it for four intermittently numbing years in exile. I had even started running again, running on the Chesapeake beach or along the state-park bike path most mornings before heading off to my job in Norfolk.

In the midst of such bounty and such promise, and provoked by nothing I could name, I suddenly thought what might seem like a strange thought under the circumstances. At the age of forty, I had accomplished only this: I saw how far I had gotten off track.

It was as if those difficult years in Texas had somehow distracted me from seeing that the real work—the interior work—was being neglected. And, to be honest, my difficulty with a handful of colleagues there and a regrettable lack of humility on my part had led me to speak and act in ways I knew, even at the time, to be wrong, ways that ate at me still.

Shame is a curious phenomenon. It can provoke further, entrenched, and shameful response—compounding the shame, compounding the poor response, ad infinitum—or like a sharp and stinging wind it can startle even the dullest of us into repentance. Now that my job was once again rewarding, now that my family was safe and happy, I relaxed enough to glimpse a subtle reality: I saw how far I stood from where I'd meant to be by now.

Rather, I saw how far I stood from where I'd meant to be by *then*.

I have recently turned fifty. And though it is possible that some progress has been made in the intervening ten years of *meantime*, that progress has been very slow, negligible, and remarkably unsteady, with virtually every advance being followed, hard on the heels, by an eclipsing retreat—with hard words, harsh thoughts, continuing to undermine any accomplishment in the realms of charity and compassion.

In his Christmas oratorio, *For the Time Being*, the beloved Mr. Auden puts it in a way that never fails to resonate with me, to slap me awake when I recite his poem (which I do as a matter of course every Christmas Eve): "To those who have seen / The Child, however dimly, however incredulously, / The Time Being is, in a sense, the most trying time of all."

I get that, too.

Wise men and women of various traditions have troubled the terms *being* and *becoming* for centuries without arriving at anything like conclusion. Every so often, though, I glimpse that some of the trouble may derive from our merely being, when—as I learned to say in Texas—we *might could be* becoming.

I wonder if we aren't fashioned to be *always* becoming, and I wonder if the dry taste in my mouth isn't a clue—and even a nudge—that staying put is, in some sense, an aberration, even if it may also be a commonplace.

I have been a Christian virtually all of my life, have hoped, all of my life, to eventually find my way to some measure of . . . what? Spirituality? Maturity? Wisdom? I'd hoped, at least, to find my way to a sense of equanimity, or peace, or . . . *something*.

As one Desert Father, Abba Xanthias, observed—clearly anticipating my Labrador—"A dog is better than I am, for he has love and he does not judge."

At the age of forty, I raised my arm to fling a sodden stick into the Chesapeake; I looked down to see my beautiful, dripping yellow dog—braced, alert, eager, her eyes lit up with wild expectation. I didn't want to let her down.

My life at that precise moment reminds me of the bumper sticker I saw years ago: *I want to be the man that my dog thinks I am.*

More generally, my life at that moment reminds me of an often-repeated comment one monk made to a visitor to Mount Athos. I imagine it like this: The visitor asks what it is that the monks *do* there; and the monk, looking up from the black wool of the prayer rope he is tying, stares off into the distance for a moment, silent, as if wrestling with the answer. Then he meets the other man's eyes *very* directly and says: "We fall down, and we get up again."

A little glib, but I think I get the point.

Monks, it turns out, can seem a little glib on occasion, and I've noticed that they have a general penchant for the oblique; but I'll have more to say about that by and by.

As for me, at the moment when my brilliant day at the beach was suddenly clouded by an encroaching unease, I saw that I was less like that diligent monk, and more like the actor in the TV ad who says *I've fallen, and I can't get up.*

Even if the monk's words do offer a glimpse of a truth that is available to us all, I keep thinking that—for the saints, for the monks, for the genuinely wise, presumably for anyone but me—the subsequent fall needn't seem so completely to erase all previous progress.

I keep thinking that, for the pilgrim hoping to make any progress at all, the falling down must eventually become less, that the rising up must become something more—more of a steady ascent, and more lasting.

I also have an increasing sense that the subsequent fall need not be inevitable.

I keep thinking that this is actually possible: the proposition of spiritual development that leads us into becoming, and—as the fathers and mothers of the Eastern Christian tradition would have it—into always becoming.

The question must be how to get from here to there.

And that question has pressed me to get serious, to slap myself awake, take up my bed, and get to walking.

I hope to be, at long last, a pilgrim on the way.

—

The boat—whose name means *It Is Worthy*—is backing away from the chaos of crates and trucks and the crowd of very loud, very animated men burdening the concrete pier. With a shudder and a plume of diesel smoke, the ferry discovers a forward gear and angles out, pressing into the Aegean's dappled blue.

I was a little puzzled, at first, by the size of the crowd boarding the boat. And, a little earlier in the morning, I was a little panicked that my friend Nick and I had to wait to see if there would be room for us to join them. We had made the necessary arrangements to enter Mount Athos on this date, but hadn't known to reserve tickets for the boat itself. Let that be a lesson for somebody.

Given a well-publicized daily limit of 134 pilgrims—120 Orthodox Christians and 14 "others" who are allowed to enter the Holy Mountain—I had no idea there would be so many pressing to catch the morning ferry, easily four hundred men, probably more.

I was puzzled, as well, by the early-morning demeanor of some of my fellow travelers. Though we were embarking around 9:30 AM, a good dozen or so were sipping cans of Amstel lager, and many of them were obviously nursing serious hangovers. Not just a few seemed still to be drunk, and one was passed out between two comrades who kept him from falling over—for the most part.

The official limit of 134 men, it turns out, applies only to the uninvited. There is apparently no limit for visiting monks, Orthodox clergy, or for those pilgrims who have made arrangements to visit their spiritual fathers by invitation.

Still, those particular exceptions didn't absolutely account for the drunks.

The official limit doesn't apply to laborers either. In recent years, reconstruction support has come to Mount Athos from the European Union and from various public and private sources in predominantly Orthodox countries. Of the twenty monasteries and the dozen-plus sketes, virtually all are undergoing some degree of reconstruction and repair. Some, like Chelandári and Simonópetra, have suffered recent losses from fire, but all have suffered the toll of time. Megistis Lavra, Saint Panteleímon, and Saint Andrew's Skete, for instance, appear to have a good many more derelict structures than usable ones. A thousand years can erode a lot of stone and mortar, rot a lot of wood—even the iron-like chestnut beams and boards used for most wooden structures on the Holy Mountain. As a result, Mount Athos is occupied daily by an army of excavators, stonemasons, and carpenters; this morning, they weren't all hungover, but all bore the demeanors of men on their way to a day (or several weeks) of serious labor. I really couldn't blame them for their grim looks.

And I have to say that, progressively, during the boat ride, as the reality of Mount Athos began to weigh on my idealized, abstract expectations, I guessed that I, too, was on my way to work.

———

It wasn't until Nick and I had stowed our backpacks under our seats and were stretched out, feeling the sun on our faces, that any of this began to feel real. Nick, by the way, is Nick Kalaitzandonakes. And Nick—as you might have noticed from his substantial surname—is Greek. If you were Greek, you would also gather—also from his name— that his family originally hails from Crete. Nick is also an American, having been naturalized about fifteen years ago. He is married to the indefatigable Julie, and they have two beautiful, busy kids, Maria and Yorgo—both brilliant, and each, in his or her own way, full of beans.

Nick and I have served together on the parish council of our Saint Luke the Evangelist Orthodox Church since before it *was* a parish council, since before we even had a parish. We were just a "mission steering committee" at first, working to establish the first-ever Orthodox church in mid-Missouri. It worked out pretty well.

Nick is also a colleague at the University of Missouri, where I teach poetry writing and American literature in the English department, and where he is an agricultural economist. Nick was also, for the first five days of this first pilgrimage, my guide and translator.

So far, my Greek is very lame. As with about seven other languages, however, I maintain certain priorities. I can manage—politely even— to get myself fed in Greek. And I can order red wine—or single-malt scotch, when it's available. On this trip, I also learned how to reserve a room, pay a tab, count my change, and shove my way onto a bus. Nick, on the other hand, could help with the occasional theological discussion, and he's a pretty funny guy, to boot. Nick is also, as it happens, a pilgrim.

———

At that moment on the deck—with the breeze whipping up white caps on the Aegean, the ferry boat tooling along in what I swear was a confident, dactylic rhythm, and with the first monastic enclaves coming into view along the shore—I realized that I was *really* going to the Holy Mountain.

Mount Athos has always been a unique phenomenon, and, for most folks, it remains a downright puzzling phenomenon; its uniqueness and puzzlement are all the more pronounced in the twenty-first century, when ancient pursuits like monasticism, asceticism, and hesychasm (*EH see kazm*—that is, the pursuit of stillness) strike the modern psyche as anachronistic, extreme, and maybe a little perverse.

The monks also follow the Julian—which is to say, the "Old"— calendar, and this involves a tweaking of dates to a point thirteen days behind where you thought you were.

Think of it as a cosmic pressure to slow down—or, maybe better, as a metaphor for our failure to know, even, where we stand, or when. Then don't think about it again. The monks are, for the most part, gracious enough to suppose where and when you think you are, and will play along.

Oh, and one other thing: the clock. The hours of the day begin at sundown rather than at midnight. Not to worry; you'll catch on.

The easternmost of three peninsulas—easily the steepest and rockiest of three long fingers of steep and rocky land—reaching south into the Aegean from that region of northeastern Greece known as Halkidikí, the peninsula of Mount Athos is about thirty-four miles in length and varies between five and eight miles across, covering less than 250 square miles total; the sharply rising terrain moves precipitously from sea level to 6,700 feet, which is the summit of the Mount Athos peak itself, very near the southern tip of the peninsula.

In physical terms, then, the area of the Holy Mountain isn't much. In spiritual terms, it is immense, impossible to chart.

Archaeological evidence suggests that since as early as the second century ascetics have lived here in pursuit of prayer—in pursuit of, rather, *lives of prayer*. I'll get to what I mean by the italics soon enough. Or nearly soon enough. By and by.

Since the third century—and perhaps even earlier—ascetics desiring lives of prayer have lived in community here. Over the next seventeen hundred years, the precise number of these communities has varied, witnessing intermittent increase and decline; some documents indicate that as many as 180 such communities flourished at one point. The establishment of these communities appears to have occurred in two distinct waves, an early wave during the third through fifth centuries, and a second, more pronounced wave commencing in the tenth century (*Megistis Lavras*, founded in 963, is agreed to have been the earliest of these) and continuing into the fourteenth century.

Today there are twenty such communities recognized as "ruling monasteries"; because Mount Athos operates as a virtually autonomous political state, representatives from these twenty constitute the Holy Mountain's governing body. While seventeen are identified as Greek, one as Bulgarian, one as Serbian, and one as Russian, the Holy Mountain includes a full array of Orthodox nationalities, including good numbers of Romanian, Moldavian, Ukrainian, English, American, and Australian monks. There are also a dozen or more *sketes*; some of these are very like monasteries, but ostensibly—with a few notable exceptions—smaller. Each skete is a dependency of one of the twenty ruling monasteries, on whose lands it rests. Some, like the Romanian *Skíti Timiou Prodromou* (named after "the Forerunner," Saint John the Baptist), the Russian *Skíti Agios Andreas* (Saint Andrew's Skete), and *Skíti Profíti Ilíou* (Prophet Elias Skete), look very like full-fledged monasteries, with a central *katholikón* protected within a high-walled structure; others, including *Skíti Agias Annis* (Saint Anna's Skete) and *Nea Skíti* (New Skete), appear more like thriving residential communities spread across the steep Athonite slope, dotted with churches, chapels, and monastic *kéllia*, or cells. There are, as well, throughout the Athonite wilderness, many scattered, communal farm dwellings, *kalyves* (communal huts), *kathismáta* (smaller huts for single monks), and *hesychastería* (squat huts or simple caves etched in a cliff face for the most ascetic of hermits, an increasingly rare breed).

The twenty ruling monasteries are now all *coenobitic*, in which the monks all follow a common rule. Until recently, some were *idiorrythmic*, in which the monks pursued more individualized ascetic practice, often allowing for a more demanding rule. The idiorrythmic approach—still observed in many of the sketes and smaller dependencies—is thought by some to be an aberration of the ideal monastic community, albeit a historic necessity brought about during foreign occupation by Franks, Turks, and so on. Others understand the idiorrythmic rule of the skete to be more aptly suited to those monks who are permitted a more strenuous ascesis.

In either case, the monastic rule has always revolved around prayer. And fasting, too—but fasting as a tool assisting prayer. It is safe to say that nothing about life on Mount Athos is understood as an end in itself, and that everything deliberate about life on Mount Athos is undertaken to accommodate prayer. Prayer is undertaken to accommodate union with God—what those in the business like to call *théosis*.

We should probably stick to prayer for now, but théosis is the crux of our matter, and that is where—I pray—we will eventually arrive.

Odd as Mount Athos may appear by contemporary standards, the Holy Mountain is visited by hundreds of pilgrims every month. The generally balmy weather and calm seas of spring, summer, and fall bring boatload after boatload scrambling to visit the steep and rocky slopes, the deep forests of chestnut, pine, and juniper, and the ancient enclaves; though wintertime draws relatively fewer, they arrive daily and by the dozens even so—whenever the weather-driven surf allows the ferry boats to dock.

That is to say, year-round, pilgrims arrive at Mount Athos virtually every day, looking for something. One friend (now a novice monk at Simonópetra) told me that a good many visitors come in search of healing from serious illness—their own or that of a loved one—some arrive because their marriages are failing or have failed, some come to kick an addiction or two, and some few arrive because they are drawn to a fuller sense of prayer.

Most of them are Orthodox Christians, and most are from Greece; a good number arrive from other parts of eastern Europe, notably Romania and Russia. Concurrent with the rise of Eastern Orthodoxy in English-speaking countries, many also come from England, Australia, and North America. Many non-Orthodox arrive as well; from what I could gather, many of these are from Germany and other parts of western Europe.

As I mentioned, the daily limit for entry to the Holy Mountain is 120 Orthodox and 14 non-Orthodox men. Since a vote among resident monks in the year 1045 and a subsequent edict of Emperor Constantine in 1060, women are not allowed entry at all, ever.

This last bit seems to many—as it has seemed to me—to be the most archaic element of the entire operation, an element that, for some of us, threatens to turn *admirably quaint* into *regrettably anachronistic*, verging right up on the cusp of *damned insulting*. Granted, there are many monastic communities, East and West, that choose to limit their communities to one gender or the other; the Athonite monasteries are not unique in that respect. Many convents exclude men; many monasteries exclude women.

Be that as it may, Mount Athos is an entire peninsula, an entire monastic republic, and—some would say—the spiritual center of the entire Eastern Church. So, the exclusion of women strikes the casual observer as extreme, not just a little misogynistic. That sense is not much mitigated by the fact that this prohibition extends to female animals in general—save those among the wild animals and the countless cats who are pleased to keep both the rats and the vipers nicely in check.

Explanations abound, of course. One tradition has it that the Virgin Mary (whom, incidentally, the Orthodox call *Theotokos*, or *God-bearer*), traveling by ship with Saint John en route to visit Lazarus (then bishop of Cyprus), was blown off course, coming upon this beautiful peninsula. Moved by its beauty and isolation, the Virgin prayed to her Son that it might become hers to protect. The story goes that this was, and remains, a done deal.

Some legends include miraculous, audible warnings to historical female visitors—one of them being the stepmother of Muhammad the Conqueror; she had come to return the gifts of the Magi to the Christians near the site of today's monastery of Saint Paul (where those relics are now kept). By and large, the legends share one element: women are not to come here, and if they *do* come here, they shouldn't plan on sticking around.

My own guess is that the *lives of prayer* these men seek to acquire are understood by them to be more possible in an environment where certain long-standing human failures—pride, greed, violence, lust, and so on—are mitigated by a lack of opportunity. The absence of women effectively takes at least one species of error off the table, and indirectly protects the monks from a good many others. Call it self-defense against certain aspects of the self.

That said, notable exceptions have been made in the past. In particular, during the Greek civil war—which occurred in the aftermath of World War II—the monasteries of Mount Athos offered sanctuary to many women and girls fleeing the brutality of mainland atrocities. The monks made places for them, saw that they were fed, and kept them safe for the duration of the hostilities. When, back on the mainland, the coast was clear, the monks promptly cleared the Athonite coast of women.

I hoped to ask, at one point or another, about this continuing prohibition of what are, generally speaking, my favorite people. I hoped to hear an explanation that didn't sound quite so specious as the ones I'd heard so far. Mostly, I hoped at some point even to understand it, suspecting that, as with a good many things, the business might look different from the inside than it does from the outside.

————

On the *Áxion Estín*, leaning into the headwind at the bow, I was waking to the fact that Nick and I, after many months of planning and anticipation, would soon be inside, setting foot on land blessed by centuries of prayer—genuine prayer, prayer of a sort I could only suspect, and desire.

Soon, I'd be walking through what the Orthodox call "the garden of the Theotokos."

I hoped, moreover, to come upon a holy man, an adept, a spiritual father, who could help me to pray.

It was more than a little daunting.

In a curious and surprising way, the bleary-eyed stonecutter slumped next to me, picking at the bandage on his knuckle, became something of a comfort.

2

Lord, he said, teach us to pray.

Before this, my only experiences with the Holy Mountain had come through texts—ancient and modern—and through an abundance of imagery—both verbal and photographic—found on the Internet. My expectations, therefore, were guarded. I knew that many holy men had lived here over the centuries, and I knew enough to suspect that many holy men still did. I didn't expect to find a *staretz* exactly, but I did hope to find a spiritual guide—someone farther along the journey than I, someone who might help me to pray, as it were, always.

From the boat, the first monastic structures that came to view were small, discreet hermitages.

Actually, these first structures were but the *ruins* of small, discreet hermitages.

In the days ahead, similar ruins, scattered along the shores and along the remote footpaths, would do their peculiar work on me, deepening my sense of how long men had struggled here, and making palpable an ascetic isolation that has endured here for more than fifteen hundred years.

As more current structures—a white stone hut surrounded by olive groves—came into view, I took a new position, leaning over the shoreward guardrail to take it all in. The first actual monastery along the shore was Docheiaríou. It was huge, a mass of incongruent structural shapes—wooden constructions perched atop and overhanging a variety of soaring stone battlements, centuries of add-ons—from the midst of which the dome and cross of the *katholikón*, the central church, stood out, overshadowed by a tall stone tower commanding the upslope side.

Nick and I stayed on the upper deck to watch as the *Áxion Estín* pulled in to Docheiaríou's *arsanás*, its seaport. On the concrete pier, a middle-aged man in street clothes was bowing to kiss the hand of a white-haired monk. Before the pilgrim turned to hop onto the ferry's iron ramp, the two embraced warmly, kissing each other on both cheeks, embracing once again.

This scene was a little unsettling. I was, at once, both warmed and—regrettably—a little envious. This pilgrim *had* a spiritual father.

This curious mix of responses was my first taste of one of the great paradoxes of a visit to the Holy Mountain: on Athos, everyone is sure to be confronted, simultaneously and repeatedly, with the opportunity either to be his best or to be his worst.

Our next stop was Xenofóndos, a soaring expanse of stone and wooden structures behind and perched atop a granite fortress—slightly larger-seeming, slightly less incongruent in appearance than Docheiaríou—set at the very edge of the sea. From its center rose a bright yellow construction crane, indicating renovation underway. Here, the scene at the pier was repeated, except in triplicate: three pilgrims and three monks, parting with evident respect and affection. We also left six passengers on the pier—workmen, off-loading bundles of rebar and bags of cement, dragging the load to a waiting flatbed truck.

As the ferry rounded the headland to the immediate south of Xenofóndos, the immense Russian monastery of Saint Panteleímon loomed into view. In terms of scale and beauty, it is frankly astonishing. Commanding easily four times the area of Xenofóndos, the white granite battlements and rectangular buildings are capped in the center by no less that half a dozen sparkling green domes of varying size, all of them glistening as if fashioned of burnished green enamel—many of them the onion domes of the Russian tradition. Moreover, the monastery appeared once to have been far larger; four or more looming structures (each being four to six stories tall and each appearing to cover square footage exceeding that of a football field) stood without roofs or with fragments of failed roofs. Now housing about forty resident monks, the monastery was once home to nearly fifteen hundred in 1903; in the decades that followed, the Russian Revolution took its toll even here. Today (though in *my* experience they make a habit of saying they have no room available), Saint Panteleímon's can accommodate, with apparent ease, a thousand pilgrims and scholars. The *Áxion Estín* left them a good twenty, fetching away eight.

It was at this point that I sat down on a slatted bench on the sundeck and dug into my backpack for my journal. I had planned to write every afternoon, recapping the events and impressions of the previous twenty-four hours as well as I could; I'd thought to do so in the interval of quiet time before Vespers at whatever monastery I happened to be staying the night. Here I was, still on the boat at 11:00 AM of my first day, growing suddenly anxious that I would forget too much.

And there was something else: something about the presence of Saint Panteleímon monastery—its scale, its antiquity, its glistening beauty—that sparked a familiar hunger in me, a hunger *to come to terms*, if only provisional terms, with what lay before me.

Enormity is the word that came to mind just then.

Better make that *two* words—*Enormity glimpsed*.

I have often startled to a fleeting sense—either within an expanse of landscape or, for that matter, poring over a written page—that there dwells before me an excess, abysmal, roiling beyond what can be grasped. Such a sense is what first led me, even as a child, to savor the language of the Bible.

It is what first led me to the language of poetry as well.

Along the way, I've come to the opinion that *the real*—whatever that may eventually prove to be—will appear, inevitably, as abysmal.

From what I gather, I'm not alone. The general consensus of modern philosophy is that the human circumstance—duly appraised—is unquestionably abysmal. Where I might tweak the consensus view is simply here: I'm guessing that our circumstance—the abyss in which *we live and move and have our being*—need not be apprehended as an abysmal emptiness so much as an abysmal fullness.

An Enormity, I'd say.

Of which, incidentally, the human person is to become a part, a member. Appalling, yes? And abysmal. Cheerfully so, I think.

Still and in the meantime—however one might choose to speak of the accompanying sensations—our glimpses of the real are pretty much guaranteed to be vertiginous; and any taste one might have for that sensation is admittedly an acquired taste.

I have been working to acquire that taste for a long time now, going on most of thirty years.

Poetry—when it is actually poetry—suits that taste. Sacred texts—when they are pored over and pressed for unexpected and generative meaning—also serve. An expanse of landscape—whether scored and moved by human agency or by more natural activity—can also provide a savory moment availing what cannot be held.

So, as the *Áxion Estín* pushed back from the concrete pier at the foot of the immense monastery of Saint Panteleímon, I had myself another little taste.

And I opened my journal in hopes of *coming to terms*—if provisional terms—with this sense of enormity.

I wrote awhile, or tried to write, glancing up every minute or so to scan the shore as we passed along its edge, the steeply rising slope, the juniper and cypress, the ubiquitous olive groves, and countless white stone ruins.

I scribbled a load of glib banalities off and on for the next several minutes, then realized what I was doing and slammed the notebook shut.

Nick brought me another coffee, and we sipped, sighing audibly, relishing the final leg of our ferry ride as we pushed toward the tiny port of Dáfni, where we'd be getting off the boat.

——— *The Port Village of Dáfni* ———

Pilgrims are a funny bunch, a fairly mixed bag.

In the packed space of our corner on the ferry's upper deck, we witnessed a curious array. Besides the pockets of day laborers sipping beers, there were men of all shapes, sizes, degrees of facial hair—alone or in small groups—and sporting a wide range of demeanors. Throughout the two-and-a-half-hour ride, some had been playing cards or snapping the worry beads of their *komvoloi* back and forth, some had been fingering the knots of their prayer ropes while they prayed, and some were munching on Greek pastries or loosely packed sandwiches, yukking it up with their friends. Most were drinking coffee, albeit *cold* coffee, a whipped, wake-up confection made with instant Nescafe, sugar, and condensed milk that the Greeks call a Frappé; it's actually better than it sounds, as it would have to be.

Most on board were chain-smoking cigarettes, and I had gotten a pretty good nicotine buzz off the secondhand smoke. A cloud of Aegean gulls and sandwich terns had trailed the boat most of the way, and many on board were tossing them torn-off bits of breakfast; quite a few were teasing the birds to get close enough to photograph their being hand-fed, resulting in a number of nipped fingers. Everyone without a beer seemed to have a camera. Several sported a coffee in one hand and a camera in the other, sipping and snapping in intervals. One unusually tall man with a buzz cut wore what looked like an oddly orange *kaffiyeh* around his neck; he spent the boat trip lounging across a bench, playing a Jew's harp, oblivious to the lot.

The pilgrims were giddy; the day laborers, nearly sullen. Me? I was about as awake as I have ever been, feeling the cool morning air against my face, leaning ahead into what was coming, soaking up every possible detail along the way.

As Nick and I prepared to disembark at Dáfni, we hauled our gear to the iron stairway descending back to the main deck, and I was nearly sent tumbling down the steps by two young men pushing ahead. A young monk grabbed my arm so I could steady my heavy backpack and regain my balance. When I said, "Thanks," he blinked, surprised at my English. Then he smiled.

He fairly shouted, "*Welcome meester!*"

———

I had planned to be fairly deliberate about the moment of my arrival on the Holy Mountain, had planned, even, to attend with reverence to my first steps from the boat's iron ramp to the dock. As it happened, I was too busy staying on my feet; by the time I was thinking again, Nick and I had been moved by the pressing herd a good fifty yards in the direction of two idling buses that would haul us up and over the steep ridge to Karyés.

At that point, I *did* manage to slip to the side, take a deep breath, and look around. For all the bustle and confusion, the moment was sweetened when I noticed a monk with snow-white beard and hair, sitting in a corner of the café patio, eyes on the *komvoskíni* he was fingering, knot by knot. His lips were moving.

Even here—it appeared—in the most distracting spot on the Holy Mountain, a man might pray. As I rejoined the cattle drive, I gave it a try myself.

———

The bus was awash in dust, smelling of dust, tasting of dust, packed with sweating, dusty pilgrims. The windows, also dust-caked, were impossible to see through clearly; still, as we made the climb from Dáfni to Karyés, I was able to glimpse occasional dwellings, the odd monk trekking along the road, and quick takes of the glittering sea below. Within thirty minutes or so, we topped the ridge and descended into the broad valley that cradles Karyés, the governmental center of the Holy Mountain—and undeniably the *second* most distracting spot on the Holy Mountain. As our bus rattled over a bridge at the edge of town, I was surprised to see what looked to be an immense and abandoned monastery to the left of the road. I opened my map to see what it was, and learned that this was Saint Andrew's Skete, a dependency—a *metóchion*—of Vatopédi monastery.

———— *Saint Andrew's Skete* ————

I had read a bit about Saint Andrew's; originally a Russian skete, it was abandoned early in the twentieth century, largely a result of the Russian Revolution, and had only recently been reoccupied by a handful of monks from Philothéou. The new tenants also run a boarding school there for boys from mainland Greece—something of a prevocational seminary. Nick and I made a note to check out the skete on our way back through. We would be heading in the opposite direction today, walking to Philothéou itself.

Soon thereafter, the bus pulled into a very large parking lot in Karyés, where, once more pressing through a very pushy crowd, we collected our bags from beneath the bus, and made our way toward the center of town.

Until recently, pilgrims to Athos were relatively few. And the only motor vehicle available to them was along this single, decrepit bus route that would haul them from Dáfni to Karyés. From there everyone had to hoof it, walking the (mostly) cobbled footpaths—*monopathi*—from one community to the next. Hardly a week goes by, these days, when I don't come upon yet another essay, article, or letter bemoaning the "improvements," an ease of travel that has brought with it, allegedly, a surfeit of tourists and a dearth of actual pilgrims.

Most pilgrims, this day, were hurrying directly from the large buses to find seats within the fleet of microbuses and vans that would fetch them to their various monasteries.

Nick and I had planned all along to walk to Philothéou, our stop for the first two nights; in fact, it was with some measure of pride that we reported as much when asked—and we were asked this repeatedly. We bumped and angled through the crowd of pilgrims and the gauntlet of drivers—who at the moment seemed very like carnival barkers—and toward what appeared to be the heart of the village.

Once free of the crowd and in the relative calm of the nearly vacant square, we discovered a renewed sense of having arrived. We stood in the narrow, cobbled road between shops, and looked at each other grinning. Nick said, "Hey, we're really here!"

Then we hunkered down at the side of the road to consult the map, just to be sure we knew where *here* was.

Like most *diamonitíria*—the official documents permitting entry to Mount Athos, and, without which, you won't so much as get a foot on board the ferryboat—ours had been issued for a four-day visit. Our plan was for the two of us to spend a couple days and nights at Philothéou, where a family friend of Nick's served as second to the abbot; we would then decide where to spend the next two days, after which Nick would leave for Athens, and I would continue my pilgrimage alone. As I hoped to stay another six or seven days beyond the first four, I would need an extension of my diamonitírion. Karyés is the place to do this, so we ducked into one of the several shops to ask which building held the office I needed. The shopkeeper, Dimitri, was happy to help; as we lowered our packs, he even offered us cold water and *loukoúmi*—known outside of Greece as Turkish delight. Walking us down the cobbled road a few meters past his shop

window, he pointed across the road to the *Protaton* (First One)—
the tenth-century church that continues to serve the community of
Karyés—and the yellow government building nestled on the slope to
the right of it.

We hurried up the steps to see about my extension, but were met at
the door by half a dozen Athonite police in dress uniform and several
suspiciously hierarchical monks in full array. For all we knew, this was
how these guys dressed all the time, so we started to slip by them to enter
the building. With a tone that sounded very like anger to me (though
Nick assured me it was more nearly surprise at our foolishness), one of
the police officers asked us where we thought we were going.

Nick explained our purpose, and the officer—still shouting and
speaking very quickly—said we'd have to come back tomorrow.

Turns out, the patriarch of Alexandria—the hierarch of the entire
church of Africa—was at that moment making his way by helicopter
to the Holy Mountain accompanied by several other African bishops
and their attendants—a party of fifteen, plus a couple pilots. This was,
of course, a *very* big deal, while one American pilgrim arranging an
extension was clearly not. I would have to travel back this way before
my first four days were up.

We went back to Dimitri's shop to fetch our backpacks, and to get
directions for the two-hour hike to Philothéou.

"You're walking?" Dimitri asked, incredulous.

"Well, yeah. Isn't that the best way to see Mount Athos?" I asked.

He smiled, "It's the best way to see a lot of Athos that you hadn't
counted on."

He suggested we might want to rethink our plans and travel via
microbus; he insisted that the *monopáthi*, the footpaths, were very
confusing unless you've been down the trails before. When we
insisted that we wanted to walk, he just shrugged, then encouraged
us to stay on the road, which was more likely to get us there than
the monopathi, none of which were well marked. He was smiling—
maybe even shaking his head a little—as we said our good-byes and
headed out.

The day was very warm—well over ninety degrees—but the shaded trail beneath the canopy of chestnut trees was remarkably cool, the air spiced with honeysuckle, chestnut, and pine. The trail at this point was actually cobbled, and foot-worn stones of granite and marble stretched far into the chestnut forest.

I couldn't keep from grinning. I was walking where actual saints had walked, men whose memory we keep as part of the liturgical life of the church, Saint Gregory Palamás himself, Saint Sílouan, Saint Nikódemos, Saint Sávas, and dozens of other beloved saints, as well as countless holy men whose names are known only to God. In retrospect, it may seem a little silly—at least sentimental—but for much of that first hour, I kept my eyes for the most part on my boots as they munched along that path, clamoring along the very stones that holy men had walked upon, stones that holy men had long ago set in place. And I said the prayer as I walked.

The prayer is the Jesus Prayer. And it is as simple as can be.

It's most lengthy version is a mere twelve words: *Lord Jesus Christ, Son of God, have mercy on me, a sinner.*

Other forms are simpler yet. Some practitioners say only *Lord Jesus Christ, have mercy on me.* Some, on occasion, say, simply, *Jesus,* the form recommended by one of my favorite modern authors on the subject, Father Lev Gillet, known more widely by his nom de plume, "A monk of the Eastern Church."

The issue, in any case, is to repeat the prayer, not so much to invoke Christ's presence—which, one comes to understand, is unfailingly *here*—as to accustom our own hearts to an awareness of that presence—always.

This tradition, as it has developed, is the Christian East's response to Saint Paul's charge, recorded in his first letter to the Thessalonians, that believers "pray without ceasing."

The resulting tradition is one that, over the centuries, developed as a practice by which Christians—of any stripe, frankly—might actually be able to do what they're told, might accomplish the astonishing admonition to pray "ceaselessly." What the Fathers and Mothers of the Church learned along the way was this: an established practice of deliberate, overt repetition of the prayer leads to the establishment of a habitual, internal repetition, and that repetition—this is the kicker—trains the one who so prays to be increasingly aware of God's unfailing presence.

This awareness, it so happens, is the gate swinging open to the kingdom of God, here and now.

We often speak, more or less carelessly, about God's nearness, as if this nearness were ever anything but absolute. If we took a little more care with our language—more care with how and what we read, write, and speak—we might better understand that the issue has less to do with God's drawing nigh, and everything to do with the degree of our own apprehension of what is always so: His absolute proximity. He is nearer, always, than our breaths; without His constant Presence and Agency, we would cease to be. Those moments when He seems far away are the moments when our own, solipsistic delusions are in full force and dim the eye.

There is, of course, a lot more to it than that, but let's leave the matter there for the time being. This provocative tradition—the Jesus Prayer—is also widely known as the prayer of the heart.

———

My own meandering path to the Jesus Prayer began in late 1974, when, as a college freshman, I read J. D. Salinger's novel *Franny and Zooey* over Christmas break. That novel happens to be about a young woman suffering what I would now recognize as a spiritual crisis.

At that time I, too, was experiencing something of a crisis. In my first semester at college, I was trying to sort through some of the untenable baggage of my belief without abandoning the faith altogether. In the midst of that crisis, I took to reading.

In the midst of *her* crisis, Franny is depicted as clutching a "small pea-green clothbound book" and moving her lips soundlessly. We don't learn until relatively late in the novel what that book is or what she is doing. The pea-green book, as it turns out, is *The Way of a Pilgrim*, and the lovely Franny—with whom, incidentally, I fell in love as I read the book—is saying the Jesus Prayer.

Salinger's novel—that is, his character Zooey, Franny's brother—presents a fair synopsis of this little book in Franny's hands, and that synopsis piqued my interest enough to read *The Way of a Pilgrim* for myself soon thereafter. When I did so, I discovered that the "pilgrim" of the title was himself something of a reader, and a diligent one at that. He wandered the steppes of Russia praying and reading; he was also, intermittently, pursued by wolves, persecuted unjustly, befriended or mugged or exploited by a wide array of proximate Russian folk, and mentored by a bona fide *staretz*—that is, he was guided in his successful journey to prayer by a holy man, an adept at the Jesus Prayer. In his backpack, the pilgrim carried only "rusks of bread," and, in the breast pocket of his cloak, he carried two books: the Holy Bible and a copy of something called *The Philokalía*.

Well, I knew of the Holy Bible, sure enough, but I didn't know beans about *The Philokalía*, hadn't so much as heard of it—and I certainly didn't know how to pronounce it (*fee lo kah LEE ah*, in case you're wondering). Mostly, I was puzzled by what I perceived to be its centrality to the staretz, to the pilgrim, and to the Jesus Prayer tradition they represented. In the words of the staretz:

> The sun is the greatest, most brilliant, most excellent luminary of the heavens, but you cannot attend it with the naked eye. You need a piece of treated glass, which, though a million times smaller and duller than the sun, allows you to examine this magnificent emperor of the heavenly luminaries—admire it, and attract its fiery rays. In the same way, Sacred Scripture is a brilliant sun and *The Philokalía* is the necessary piece of glass which enables our access to the most sublime source of light.

The Philokalía (a richly chewy Greek title that, roughly translated, indicates in one economical package a love of the good, the beautiful, the exalted) is a compilation, a gathering together of otherwise discrete writings by a wide array of holy men—monks for the most part. The title itself was first coined by two famous Cappadocians—Saints Basil the Great and Gregory of Nazianzus—as the title for their own careful selection of the works of one unjustly assailed Origen. Over subsequent centuries, the word was recycled as a fitting title for subsequent other collections of works written to assist spiritual practice.

The earliest texts included in what *we* now call *The Philokalía*— those attributed to the solitaries, Saint Isaiah and Evagrios—were written in the fourth century, and the latest were written in the fifteenth. Most were written originally in Greek, but two—those written by Saint John Cassian and Saint Gregory the Great—were originally composed in Latin. All were gathered into a Greek-language edition by Saint Nikódimos of the Holy Mountain (that is, of *Mount Athos*) and Saint Makários of Corinth, and published in Venice in 1782. Soon thereafter, the staretz Paisii Velichkovski, an Athonite monk who had left Mount Athos to serve as abbot of the Neamtu monastery in Moldavia, translated sections of that work—along with a couple very worthy additions—into the Slavonic version, *Dobrotolubiye*. First published in Moscow in 1793, this *Dobrotolubiye* is the edition pored over by our pilgrim as he wandered the Russian steppes on his journey to ceaseless prayer.

From the original Greek edition, a full, five-volume Russian translation was made by Saint Theophan the Recluse and, beginning in 1877, was published serially on Mount Athos, at the Russian monastery of Saint Panteleímon. G.E.H. Palmer and E. Kadloubovsky brought out a selective English translation of the Russian text in 1951. In 1979, Palmer, Bishop Kallistos Ware, and the poet and translator Philip Sherrard began publishing their English translations of the original Greek text compiled by Saints Nikódimos and Makários; four of the five proposed English volumes are available in that series today.

This version of *The Philokalía*—the one you can get your hands on—offers both a developmental history of the Jesus Prayer tradition and many centuries of practical assistance to the pilgrim who would learn to pray—whether he or she sets out on that journey at the age of forty, or fifty, or any age.

———

But back to the prayer itself, the prayer of the heart.

I said above that it is a very simple prayer; but, to be fair, it is also laden with complexity. Many Fathers and Mothers of the Church have observed that it contains—in its few words—the whole of the Scriptures. Some have said, similarly, that it contains all theology in a nutshell. At the very least, it holds the core of Orthodox Christology. The believer who prays *Lord, Jesus Christ, Son of God* has already made a powerful confession, affirming both the concurrent human lordship—the God-to-man, condescending anointedness of Jesus—*and* his innate divinity. The man or woman who speaks the prayer is also invoking the holy name itself—*Jesus*, a name which is, as we say, above all others, the name of the one by whom all humanity, forever, partakes of divinity and is healed of spiritual death, pretty much regardless of their noticing.

The second half of the prayer, the petition proper, is no less laden with import, and no less allusive to scriptural prototype. *Have mercy on me, a sinner* brings together the pleas of the publican, the thief, the leper, and the blind man. *Have mercy on me, a sinner* both bears and *bares* a hidden truth; it also—quite expediently—owns up to it.

Saint Hesychíos, one of my favorites among the fathers of the *Philokalía*, writes, "With every rainfall, the earth grows softer; just so, the Holy Name of Christ increasingly softens the heart, gladdens it with every prayer."

———

I should say a little something here about the prayer rope—the *chótki* for the pilgrim of *The Way of a Pilgrim* and the *komvoskíni* for the Greek monks on Mount Athos. Whether or not you would recognize them, you may have seen them, even in America. If you are Orthodox, you may even wear one, or know folks who do; it's very likely that they're available in your parish bookstore, on your parish book table.

I can't be sure, but I think that I saw one hanging from the left wrist of actor Tom Hanks during a *Late Show* appearance with David Letterman. Honest.

They are, commonly, black wool, tied in strings of thirty-three, or fifty, or a hundred or more hard, square knots (sometimes wooden beads), usually held together in a loop by a cross-shaped gathering of knots and a tassel.

The knots or beads are for focusing on repetitions of the prayer.

The cross is kissed reverently at the beginning and the end of each cycle through the rope.

The tassel is for wiping your tears, which, if you're lucky, will eventually accompany your prayer.

Using a prayer rope is not essential in the practice of the Jesus Prayer, but it helps. Focusing on moving your thumb and forefinger from one knot to the next actually assists in focusing on the words of the prayer, mostly because this simple activity of the hand helps keep the mind from wandering elsewhere. This is but one example among many, I suppose, of the Eastern Church's insistence that the attitude and activity of the body are not unrelated to the actions of the soul.

Other examples of what I think of as the *full-body faith* include making the sign of the cross; "venerating" the cross, the icons, and the relics with a bow and an actual kiss; and making full prostrations during private prayer, and even—during certain prayers and hymns of Lenten and Holy Week services—making those prostrations publicly.

In general, Christians in the West can be a little slow to appreciate the full-body character of Orthodox worship; in my own case, a lifelong habit of living in my head—approaching prayer as if it were a species of thought—had reinforced a sense that faith was an idea—a really good idea, granted, but primarily an activity of the mind.

The Church in the East has taught me, albeit very slowly, that the Christian faith is not at its core a propositional faith; Christianity is not, finally, about what we think. It is about what we are, and what we are becoming. It is necessarily an embodied, a lived faith, just as God's love is necessarily an embodied, enacted love, an incarnation.

In the early Church, the words for practice (*praxis*) and faith or vision (*theoria*) were understood as distinct terms for two things that could, frankly, never occur separately—or, as Saint James so aptly puts it: faith without works is dead.

Small as it is, the prayer rope does its bit to re-*pair* the inherited schism within the human person, helps to connect the actions of the mind with the actions of the body, helps, even—in the words of Saint Isaak of Syria—to bring the mind *into* the heart.

In *The Way of a Pilgrim*, the pilgrim—grieving for his failure to acquire a reliable habit of prayer—complained that "at first it seemed as if things were moving along. Then a great heaviness, sloth, boredom, and drowsiness began to overcome me, while a mass of thoughts closed in like a storm cloud." To this plea, the staretz replied: "Take this chótki and use it while you repeat the prayer . . . whether you are standing, sitting, walking, or lying down, continue to repeat: 'Lord Jesus Christ, have mercy on me!' Do not speak loudly, do not rush, but without fail repeat it three thousand times each day, neither increasing nor decreasing this number on your own. Through this exercise, God will help you to attain the unceasing prayer of the heart."

The number of repetitions, according to tradition, matters far less than simple obedience to a rule. I say *simple*, but it is absolutely the key, this obedience. Certain novice monks of Mount Athos begin with but a thousand repetitions. And there are abundant warnings that, while anyone can benefit from a rule of repetition, excessive repetitions without the assistance of a guide will most often lead to discouragement and failure.

The pilgrim continues, "The elder sent me away, giving me his blessing. He told me that while learning this prayer I should come often to him to reveal my thoughts in honest confession; to arbitrarily take up the prayer without conversation with a guide would be unwise, bringing little success."

So, back to my journey.

That I am a sinner is no great surprise, as, I'm sure, that it is no surprise to anyone who knows me. That I might ask for mercy has been also a long-held, long-embraced comfort. That I might become less of a sinner, less distracted, less broken, and more Christlike (but never seemed to do so) has been the nagging thorn of my life to date, pricking at my heart during my stillest moments—even and especially during prayer itself.

This disparity was the focus of my trouble that day on the Chesapeake beach, and it has become the escalating chagrin of the nearly ten years composing the interim.

Unlike, say, the Sunday-school teachers of my youth, I wasn't so much concerned with being saved from hell as I was with being saved from habit.

Could be what I needed was a guide.

3

so great a cloud of witnesses

Along the trail to Philothéou, the trail skirted a small stone hut—with granite walls and a heavy slate roof—clearly ancient, abandoned, sunken under centuries of weather. The melancholy of the anonymous life (or series of lives) spent here—solitary, uncelebrated, and full of ceaseless toil—struck me speechless. Nick wasn't saying much either.

The prayer of the heart—it is said—brings solace, and a peace that surpasses understanding. Saint John Karpathos speaks of a "new heaven of the heart in which Christ dwells." Saint Theophan adds, "These practices, if followed even reasonably aright, will not allow you to grow despondent. For they bring spiritual consolation such as nothing else on earth can give." Passing alongside that anonymous plot, I was hoping this was so.

After about an hour of an almost hallucinatory sweetness, intermittently pressed by an almost hallucinatory melancholy, the cobbled path through chestnut forest ended at a broad road of crushed granite. The scarf of dust wafting along its surface told us that a vehicle had just passed by.

Nick and I examined the undergrowth on the other side to see if the trail picked up there, but found only brambles and a steep slope descending, and decided we should follow the road in the general direction we had been going, keeping our eyes open for any sign of the trail picking up again.

It didn't, not for a long time.

Through an effective combination of inattention, the pinching burden of heavy packs, the dearth of road signs, and the fact that—once we hit the dirt road—Nick and I hardly stopped yakking, our "two-and-a-half hour walk" from Karyés to Philothéou stretched into a six-hour slog. We got good and lost, and utterly exhausted.

The maps—we had two of them—were only moderately helpful for this stretch of road. And the lack of road signs at key intersections left us to make a series of poor guesses, and missteps. Once, early on, as we stood at a crossroads scratching our heads, a monk in a Land Rover happened by.

When greeting a monk, the convention is to say, "*Evlogíte*," which implies an imperative, something like "Bless!" to which the monk will surely respond, "*O Kyrios*," emphasizing "the *Lord* blesses." We exchanged these greetings, and Nick got the directions we needed for the moment. Still, our confidence diminished as the crossroads multiplied without any subsequent interventions.

Every step was accompanied by the thought that we would likely be retracing it after the next turn dead-ended, and we did find ourselves retracing a good number of those steps as midday wore on into late afternoon.

Also, intermittently throughout our trek, we kept hearing the sound of a helicopter circling. After the third pass over, we made jokes about it—the monks knew we were lost, and were searching for us.

Finally, at nearly 4:30 PM we came upon a signpost indicating the trail to Philothéou. Bleary-eyed, weak-kneed, and dripping wet, we snapped photographs of each other in front of that very reassuring sign.

A good hour later—a good *three* hours past when we had planned to arrive—we stumbled up the steep trail, the final slope. Absolutely spent—my back was in spasms at this point—and soaked through, we entered the clearing at the top and beheld the high walls of the monastery. By the time we had made it around to the single gateway, it was already nearly 6:00 PM, not a soul to be seen. Just inside, we saw a young monk striding our way, hurrying on his way out the gate. Nick asked him for directions to the *archondaríki*, the guesthouse; without slowing, the monk looked straight ahead and blurted something that sounded very like a Greek rendition of "ask someone who gives a damn." Nick chose not to translate.

As we eased our heavy packs to the ground in the courtyard, we heard chanting.

Hymns. Vespers, in fact. The service was well underway, so we ditched our packs just inside the low wall of the courtyard font, the *phiále*—and hurried into the katholikón.

Just as with my first steps onto the Holy Mountain, here again, circumstances had led to my rushing into an experience that, previously, I had hoped to approach with greater awareness, greater attention. And I *would* have hurried inside had the darkness not stopped me in my tracks.

This was my first experience of an Athonite church. And though I 'd entered in a state that was far from ideal—harried, hurried, confused, aching, and soaking wet—the effect was immediate and palpable. First off, as I stepped from late afternoon sun into the dark narthex I was effectively blinded. Not all the churches on the Holy Mountain are as dark as the katholikón at Philothéou, but a good many are. The combination of dark icons covering virtually every inch of every surface—a darkness made all the deeper by centuries of soot (from beeswax candles and resinous incense)—and the relatively few candles lit for this moment of the service had me standing just inside the doorway for a good sixty seconds, blinking, straining to see what was before me.

Once my eyes had adjusted, I made my way to the icons in the narthex to venerate them—that is, to approach each icon, making the sign of the cross before them; to bow, touching one hand to the floor; and to set my lips to the icon's cool surface. That's what we call veneration, honoring the Image of Christ our God in the image of the saint. In my Protestant days, I would have been uneasy about this, but back then I wasn't exactly diligent about honoring the Image of Christ our God *anywhere*, in strangers, in neighbors and friends, not even in myself. I'm getting the hang of it finally, and it started with the icons.

Visitors to Orthodox churches—both at home and here on the Holy Mountain—will no doubt feel shy about entering a strange church and strolling up to venerate the icons while the service goes on around them. That's only normal. We are—O belovéd—a self-conscious people, no? Most of us would far rather slip into strange circumstances as unobtrusively as possible.

Understood.

Still, get over it.

For the Orthodox, while it may be appear to be something of a faux pas—if a surprising commonplace—to arrive late for a service, and while it may appear to be a greater faux pas to walk up to venerate the icons while the service is well underway, it is *far* worse—you'll have to trust me on this—to enter the church without thus venerating the holy images there. If you show up late, you pretty much have a choice between two disconcerting deeds: either embarrass yourself slightly further by honoring our holy antecedents (Christ and His saints) in the midst of prayers, or shame yourself and dishonor the saints by attempting to slip in unnoticed. Embarrassment is probably better than actual shame, and way better than dim-witted disrespect.

There are, even so, certain moments in a given service when you would do well to wait a bit before wandering to the fore—during the censing of the icons, the procession or the reading of the Holy Gospel, the procession or the consecration of the Holy Mysteries—but at any other time, get yourself up there to honor those who, as we like to think of it, would pray *with you*, and unceasingly.

————

In the Baptist community in which I was raised, the idea of saints didn't figure much. In fact, the presence of these "others," my connection to them, the possibility of my communing with them, asking for their prayers—none of that made its way into my conscious life nor into my prayer. The closest I came to any such awareness during my first forty years occurred with the death of my father, when—among other, mostly puzzling emotions—I began to sense that I might keep speaking to him, even though he had, as I now think of it, fallen asleep.

A more general sense of "the presence of our belovéd departed" came about quite unexpectedly. Between my "Presbyterian period" and my "embracing the fullness of the faith," I put in some time among the Episcopalians.

When I and my family first moved to Virginia Beach, we set out to find a church—that is, a Presbyterian Church. And we visited a good many, every flavor of Presbyterianism then available in the Tidewater area of Virginia. I won't go into any great detail about that sequence of disappointments, but suffice it to say that Marcia and I never found a fit, nothing quite so right-seeming as our sweet community at Trinity Church in Denton, Texas. Personally speaking, the Presbyterian bodies in Virginia Beach felt a little too like the Baptist church of my youth—a little cranky, a little suspicious, more or less besieged.

At any rate, thanks to our Cape Henry neighbors, the Powells—Rob, Cathy, Paige, and Nancy—we found our way to All Saints Episcopal Church, where we found a generous, welcoming community and, in Father Stan Sawyer, a well-read pastor with a very welcome sense of humor.

Besides offering us our first deliberate taste of sacramental theology, the community of All Saints (whose name is, I now realize, *very* significant) supplied the occasion for my first apprehending the appalling presence of *the cloud of witnesses*, before whom we necessarily stand, regardless of our habitual obliviousness to the fact.

It happened more or less like this: I had made my way to the altar for Communion, as I had many times before. This morning, as the Eucharist was placed in my hand—as I stared at that thin wafer with sudden apprehension of what I held—I heard Father Stan say, as he had always said, "The Body of Christ."

As the cup came around, I took that wafer between thumb and finger, and dipped it into the chalice of wine, accompanied by the deacon's words: "The blood of Christ."

I placed those appalling elements on my tongue and returned to my place in the nave, where I knelt to pray, with uncharacteristic concentration. Then, though my eyes were closed, I began to notice the flickering effect caused by the passing of others who were then returning to their seats. As they walked down the aisle immediately to my right, they passed between me and the glorious stained-glass windows on the other side of the aisle, through which, all this time, brilliant sunlight was pouring. As others partook at the altar, the priest's words continued, echoing throughout the sanctuary, "The Body of Christ."

As those words resonated, I beheld the flickering shadows of those moving by my side. I startled, first, to the realization that these men, women, and children *were* the Body of Christ, and then, as suddenly, with the help of flickering shadow, I startled to the realization that these represented as well the body entire—the living and the dead, the cloud whose presence I had, until this moment, failed to acknowledge.

———

But back to the katholikón of Philothéou. Once I could see beyond my nose, I saw a great deal all at once. The first thing I registered was a lush beauty, golden surfaces, flickering candles and oil lamps, Byzantine icons reaching high along each wall and up into the overarching dome. Virtually every inch of ceiling and wall surface, from the exonarthex to the curve of wall around the altar, was covered in hand-painted iconography—beloved saints, hagiographic narratives, and biblical scenes. Most Athonite katholika are structurally similar, varying for the most part only in terms of scale and proportion, and occasionally varying in numbers of narthexes and adjacent chapels. The heart of the church is the four-columned, domed sanctuary, with a cruciform floor plan. The cross of that form is a *Greek* cross, mind you, parsed into four equal quarters—with the central entry opening at the foot of that cross.

So, imagine a huge Greek cross laid flat. Lining the outer edges of the lower leg and both arms, narrow stalls of heavy dark wood have been installed, facing, of course, into the center. Recently, my friend Stelios has helped me notice that these stalls are placed in such a way—lining the walls—that the worshipers face one another; that is, you may not always see what goes on inside the altar space, but you will nearly always see the faces of those around you.

These wooden stalls are ingeniously constructed—with seats that fold either partly or completely out of the way—to support worshipers in a variety of sitting, standing and leaning positions throughout the long services, which regularly last four to five hours, and which, during a festal vigil, often stretch well beyond eight. Remember, these are monks; they live for these prayers. The liturgical *work* of the church is their life's work.

Pilgrims generally find a stall in the area of the cross's base or in the narthex, which is also similarly lined with stalls. The monks, especially those who are actually serving—as readers, chanters, or orchestrating the candlelight—find places in the cross's twin arms, which constitute the facing *choirs* proper. Transecting the cross's upper quarter, about a third of the way up, stands the *iconostasis*, the icon-bearing wall protecting the altar area. The iconostasis has a center, double-door opening—the Royal Doors—directly before the altar, and two side doors, or deacons' doors, on either side. On Mount Athos, the oldest iconostases are constructed of intricately carved white marble or white granite, others are constructed of intricately carved wood, and most are layered in gold. Many brass candelabra, brass candle stands, and a good many icons—most especially the "miracle-working icons"—are also covered in gold. Most miracle-working icons—and each monastery has an array of these—are housed in finely wrought settings that duplicate in gold and silver the figures on the icon itself. These settings leave openings through which the faces and hands of the figures are visible.

Behind the iconostasis lies the altar—marble or wooden or golden—as well as (off to the left) the table upon which the elements are prepared before being brought to the altar for the consecration of the Holy Mysteries. In most cases, one can also glimpse an array of ancient icons keeping watch over the interior of the altar space as well.

We weren't there long before I recognized the familiar hymns that conclude the Vespers service, and as the choir sang those hymns, each of the monks filed up to venerate the central icons on his way out. When they had finished, the pilgrims followed suit.

When the monks had exited, Nick and I stood a moment not sure exactly what to do. Then we followed the last of the pilgrims and joined the monks out in the courtyard just as the bell rang out to call us to *trápeza*, the communal meal.

We learned the routine as we went. First the monks filed in, and thereafter the pilgrims, following them inside, were directed to separate tables, where bowls had already been filled and laid out at each place, along with communal bowls of olives, baskets of bread, pitchers of water, and—unless it's a day of fasting—wine. The meal was simple potatoes and fish, roasted together in olive oil and garlic. I would have licked my bowl clean if I had been alone.

The rule at trápeza is, for the most part, silence. Monks and pilgrims alike are encouraged to eat silently, thoughtfully, if at a fairly brisk pace—listening all the time to a single reader who is reading, most often, from one of the lives of the saints. If I knew a good deal more Greek, I might have gathered more from these readings; as it was, as I cleaned my bowl, sneaking looks at the monks' tables, I began to learn something of their life together.

When the meal was over, the abbot lifted a bell near his place and gave it a modest ring. On that signal, we all stood for the abbot's blessing; then, following the monks—who filed out in something resembling hierarchical order following their abbot's lead—we pilgrims filed out, leaving behind only those monks with kitchen duty to complete their work. As I approached the doorway, I realized that the abbot himself now stood to the right, bowing very low to all who exited, and I saw that, across from him, on the left, three other monks—those who had sat with him at the front table—stood as well, bowing low to those who passed between them and the abbot. As I exited through their strange gauntlet, feeling more than a little self-conscious, I saw that the abbot's hand was raised to us in a sign of blessing.

As the physically and emotionally demanding days on the Holy Mountain began to wear away at my habitual reserve, this simple, humble, and humbling gesture would actually bring an ache to the throat. It's a curious thing.

The servant of all, Jesus says, is the greatest of all. He who exalts himself shall be humbled; he who humbles himself shall be exalted. These sometimes-neglected paradoxes of the faith are simply and powerfully embodied—one might say, insisted upon—on Mount Athos. You really can't miss them.

As we entered the courtyard that first evening at Philothéou, still aching and still plenty damp from nearly six hours on the road, Nick suggested we check in with Father Iosíf, the family friend and second to the abbot of Philothéou. I tested my lower back, and felt the slight twinge that told me I should take care or suffer a spasm. I was thinking, "Just so we don't have to hike anywhere to find him."

After a little further misdirection, we found our way to his offices. We found, as well, a huddled circle of monks, all of them leaning over—curiously enough—a web page on a computer screen. One monk—looking extremely sober—was nodding slowly as he spoke into the phone. Almost on cue, they all appeared to notice us standing in the hallway, and waved us into the room. We were warmly greeted and offered seats, whereupon the circle immediately dispersed, leaving us suddenly with Father Iosíf and one assistant—the same monk who would eventually show us to our room.

We were more than a little puzzled as Father Iosíf began to express sorrow that our visit had come at such a sad time. We had no idea what he meant.

He was quiet for a moment, sat again behind his desk, then quietly told us that the patriarch of Alexandria and his party had been lost at sea when their helicopter went down.

I was certain I had misunderstood him, but Nick's response was a grim assurance: "What?" he said in English. "Today?"

During the long afternoon that Nick and I had been wandering in the general direction of the monastery, while we were, often enough, heading the wrong direction, we kept hearing the chop and thrum of a helicopter circling overhead. I remembered our joke—that the helicopter was probably searching for us.

We learned from Father Iosíf that these actually *had* been search helicopters. Within moments of our leaving Karyés—where the monastic community had been in bustling preparation to receive Patriarch Petros of Alexandria—the Chinook helicopter bringing the patriarch and his company to Mount Athos spun out of control and went spiraling down, disintegrating onto the surface of the Aegean. Patriarch Petros, Metropolitan Chrysostomos of Carthage, Metropolitan Irenaeus of Pelusim, and Bishop Nectarios of Madagascar—much of the hierarchy of the North African church—were among the seventeen souls lost at sea.

We were stunned, as had been, one supposes, the monks of Mount Athos, at least initially; but, as we spoke with the fathers about the tragedy, I couldn't get over how they seemed to be taking it. Their sorrow was evident—in their words and in their faces—but there was something else being manifested here, a something else that it would take me many more days to articulate, or even adequately to recognize. They were also—it seemed to me—glad.

Father Iosíf turned to other matters. He asked about our families, asked Nick about his older brother (a Cretan iconographer with whom Father Iosíf had attended seminary); he welcomed us warmly, and made it clear that we should stay at Philothéou as long as we wished. We had planned to stay just two nights, so that we might visit other monasteries as well.

As we were stepping to the door, Father Iosíf caught my eye and pointed to a photograph on the wall facing his deck. The photo was, quite frankly, striking; it was a simple photograph of a monk, but a monk whose eyes seemed lit up, as if he were facing the sun, or had swallowed it.

"*Yéronda Ephrém*," Father Iosíf said, with sudden affection in his voice, causing his voice, for the briefest moment, to break. He explained that the *yéronda*—the elder—was the former abbot of Philothéou, and that he had gone to America to establish monastic communities there.

The monk asked if I had ever been to Saint Anthony's monastery in Arizona, where the belovéd yéronda now lived and served.

I admitted that I had not, and even as I spoke those words I had an acute sense that I was confessing something of an embarrassment, an incongruity. By coming first to Mount Athos, I had disregarded the local in favor of the exotic, ignored the near in favor of the far. And it's not as if I hadn't heard of the Yéronda Ephrém and his monastery; back home, in fact, our parish chanter, Seraphima—a woman who lives, essentially, a monastic life among us—had spoken of this very man. He was, in fact, *her* spiritual father, and a man she had come to count on for help with her own life of prayer.

Father Iosíf's eyes fixed briefly on the photograph, and in that moment, seeing the slightest tremor near the corner of his mouth, I made a note to speak to Seraphima about her elder soon as I got back home.

———— Karakálou Monastery ————

———— Philothéou Monastery Exterior ————

———— The Katholikón of Philothéou ————

4

In the early watches of the night . . .

Our small room at Philothéou—holding but two narrow beds and a bare table—overlooked the monastery's timber yard, several acres of chestnut logs stacked high and awaiting transport to Dáfni. Dusk was settling in quickly, and though it had been a hot day the wind was picking up, blowing a chill into the room through the open window. Our damp clothes didn't help matters, so we changed into dry T-shirts and jeans, and we settled in, speaking little, puzzling over the strange events of a very long day. It seemed that we had left Ouranoúpoli weeks ago.

We were also deeply exhausted, our backs in knots. Nick dug into his pack for the ibuprofen; we dosed up mightily, then turned out the lights, and I was asleep in about a minute, the words of the Jesus Prayer on my lips.

At midnight I woke to leg cramps and cold; the single blanket on the bed wasn't nearly enough. Shivering in the darkness, I felt through my pack for another shirt and for my rain parka, and I put them on. As I was doubling up my blanket, I startled to the realization that the prayer was still on my lips, still moving through my mind. I may have been shivering and wincing from muscle spasms, but in that moment I was about as happy as ever, maybe happier, to discover that the prayer was beginning to take hold. Finally.

I was still praying, though also grinning, as I warmed up, gradually stopped shivering, and dozed off again.

Shortly after 2:00 AM, I was awakened by a curious clatter—a rhythmic, staccato hammering on wood. It was the sound of the *sémantron* or, as some call it, the *tálanton*, a long board of cured chestnut wood, carved to provide a handgrip in the center and a resounding doughnut of hardwood carved at each end. This is rhythmically whacked with a mallet by the monk assigned to wake the community and to call the other monks (most of whom are already awake and praying in their cells at this hour) to prepare for midnight services.

This rhythmic hammering commences about forty-five minutes before the service begins, concluding with a single, hard whack at the end of the rhythmic riff. Thirty minutes later, the rhythm will be repeated, concluding with *two* whacks, a spondee indicating that services will begin in half an hour. A final riff begins roughly fifteen minutes later, concluding with *three* sharp whacks. For the slow pilgrim who is more than a little out of his element and suffering exhaustion, this sequence can serve, it turns out, like the snooze button on an alarm clock.

Fifteen minutes later, give or take, a similar rhythm is articulated on the *bílo*, a horseshoe-shaped iron bar, sounding very like a mid-pitched bell, announcing the actual beginning of the prayers. No more snoozing. Get to church.

———

If the dark enclosure of the narthex had been hard to navigate when we'd entered for Vespers the previous afternoon, it was abysmally difficult now—a sea of black. I pushed open the heavy wooden door to enter, and had the strange sensation that the door was still closed. I reached one hand into the void and stepped forward. In the far left corner, near the icon of the Theotokos, a single oil lamp offered a meager bead of amber light. I waded uncertainly toward it through the murk, and as I did my eyes dilated just enough for me to observe that I was not alone. Most of the stalls lining the three walls of the narthex were already occupied by monks, seated and praying, though some seemed to slump so low in their stalls—a blur of ink in the midst of deep shadow—that I wondered if they might have been sleeping there. As I reached the lampstand, my eyes had adjusted enough that I could see that the monk directly to my left was gripping a long black prayer rope, and that its knots were being drawn slowly between his thumb and fingers at a steady clip.

Wherever I worship—at my home parish, visiting in another parish, or, as it turns out, even on Mount Athos—I always light three candles, praying, as I light each, for my wife, our daughter, our son. I lit three candles with the oil lamp's flame and set them in the stand, then venerated the icons in the narthex, and entered the sanctuary.

Here again, the darkness was a little daunting—one oil lamp about twenty feet away, near the festal icon to the right, and one near the icon of the Theotokos on the left. I moved from right to left, venerating each of the icons in turn, and found a niche behind the semicircle of stalls constituting the left-hand choir, peering over the backs of the stalls to where the reader was arranging on the chanters' stand the several books he would be using during the services.

Back home, I'm usually the one who reads these particular psalms— the six psalms of *orthros*—at our Saint Luke's Parish, so the fact of their being intoned in Greek was not so great a liability; in fact, I savored the wash of sound, knowing, fairly well, their import, but hearing, as well, a mysterious otherness attending their being sung this way, as if in that confusion of sounds they became less like petitions and more like communion—that is, more nearly occasions of prayer.

These prayers began a little before 3:00 AM. They would continue— with the midnight office blending into orthros, blending into the hours, the typica service, and leading into the Divine Liturgy—until nearly 8:00 AM. Early in the midnight office, I began to notice a troubling phenomenon that would attend me intermittently through virtually every katholikón service of this first pilgrimage: I kept seeing things.

Actually, what I saw were people—people who, I'm fairly certain, were not there.

Every time I'd shut my eyes—which happened fairly often, given that this was all happening in the middle of the night, in a vertiginous, dark vault, during chanted services that stretched on for hours—it appeared that someone was standing before me, facing me, and, I think, speaking. I would startle, open my eyes, and find no one there—only the monks, the other pilgrims, and the dark expanse of the katholikón seeming to spin as the prayers continued.

Minutes later, I would close my eyes, and someone—the same figure? someone else?—would be standing before me, speaking. I could never quite tell what was said. I don't think I ever exactly recognized the speaker. I could not even say that it was always the same person. On some few of those occasions, I seemed to be facing an entire crowd, all of them speaking at once.

What should I make of this? The odds are pretty good that under the demanding conditions of these midnight prayers—for which I was, clearly, not yet prepared—I was simply falling into something approaching a dream state as soon as I closed my eyes. That's what I am thinking to make of it now—that my subconscious was uncommonly active under these rarefied circumstances.

Still, at the time, it was more than a little unnerving, and set me all the more earnestly into saying the prayer. This phenomenon would continue, off and on, throughout my first pilgrimage. Only toward the end of this first trip—after the seventh or eighth day—was I able to more or less calmly observe my visitor or visitors with something approaching dispassion, then open my eyes, returning to the service and to my prayer within it. The experience would become less frequent, less intense, with subsequent visits to the Holy Mountain, but I never have shaken the feeling that, especially within the vaults of the expansive katholika, the very air of Mount Athos is full, heavy-laden with presence. It is, in short, a place where the "cloud of witnesses" is powerfully apprehensible, palpable, welcoming—seeming to breathe and pray the endless liturgy along with those of us who intermittently happen by to join them.

———

Here, as with the celebration of the Divine Liturgy throughout the world, the seamless transition from the preparatory services to the Eucharistic service is indicated with the priest's intoning *Evlogiméni i Vasileía tou Patrós kai tou Yióu kai tou Ágiou Pnévmatos.* That is more or less to say: *Blessed is the kingdom of the Father and the Son and the Holy Spirit.*

With these words the priest announces our temporal entry into that very kingdom, and our joining, once again, in the ceaseless prayer of the angels and the saints. One of the reasons that the Orthodox, even in America, tend not to make much of a fuss over folks coming late to services—bumbling into church in the middle of things—is that, implicitly for them, once an altar is consecrated, the offering of invisible worship from that place is understood to be ceaseless. The angels and the saints—that same cloud of witness—is forever joined in concelebration. When, through *liturgía*—the work of the Church—we join *with* them, we are inevitably arriving in the middle of things.

On that first morning, as the liturgy approached its familiar focus of the Eucharist—the Holy Mysteries—I grew a little nervous. I had been looking forward to this moment—my receiving Communion on the Holy Mountain—for most of a year.

As you may or may not know, in the Orthodox Church Communion is shared from a common cup, usually a single chalice borne by a single priest. In his left hand, the priest grips the holy chalice and grips—twined between the fingers holding the cup—the corner of a scarlet cloth. In his right hand, he holds a golden spoon.

As each communicant arrives before the priest, taking one end of the scarlet cloth to hold beneath his chin, that communicant is expected to speak his or her Christian name aloud. Hearing that name, the priest says some version of "the servant of God—*insert name here*—receives the Holy Mysteries." This makes manifest an essential understanding of Orthodox faith, that we are included in mystical union with the Mystical Body of Christ, but are nonetheless ourselves, and known by name. Analogous—albeit in meager measure—to the unity of God in three persons, we share a common being without forsaking our personhood, one's *hypóstasis*.

On Mount Athos, the monks—in order of seniority—receive the Mysteries first, followed by those pilgrims who also have prepared to receive them. We had been invited with the words *Metá fóvou Theoú, písteos kai agápis, prosélthete*. With the fear of God, faith, and love, draw near.

In the eight years I had been Orthodox, I confess that certain of these words had never quite sunk in—until this moment on Mount Athos, which taught me something, in particular, of the fear of God.

As I stood behind the stalls of the left-hand choir, peering over the top at the line of monks now venerating the icons on their way to the cup, I whispered a Communion prayer, and prepared to join them. The fear of God, until this moment, had always struck me as something of an archaic cultural artifact—perhaps, even, a poor translation. I have approached with love, and with, I suppose, my own poor measure of faith; on occasion, I have approached—or have chosen *not* to approach— with shame; but fear had always proved elusive in this context.

What I learned as I approached this cup behind that line of monks and pilgrims was that this fear is real, and that it is absolutely appropriate, though it is—I should take care to point out—a very curious species of fear.

It is, I learned, a fear that draws rather than repels, a fear that trumps every other concern. In short, as I said my Christian name, *Isaák*, and as the fierce-looking priest-monk—his face made luminous by the wavering flare of beeswax candles—lifted from the golden cup an also luminous bit of wine-soaked bread upon a golden spoon, I realized that even if I had been convinced that those appalling Mysteries touching my tongue would annihilate me, I would open my mouth just the same, lean in, and partake.

I opened my mouth. I leaned in. I received the body and blood of Christ on my tongue.

And I survived.

I walked away crossing myself, a little shaken, finally tasting fear—if a new species of fear, a fear coupled with joy. Saint Isaak, my "name-saint," says, "The fear of God is the beginning of virtue, and it is said to be the offspring of faith."

If I retain nothing else from this or any journey, I hope to hold on to that fear.

For one powerful moment, I actually *had* thought those appalling Mysteries would annihilate me—which is to say, in that moment I finally believed them to be what they are. And fear was born. May virtue be its fruit.

———

The liturgy concluded with the prayers before the icon of Christ and the corporate blessing from the priest; then, lining up on our way out, we each received cubes of blessed bread, *antídoron*, from the priest's hand as he blessed us again individually.

As we walked out into the violet light of a new day, inhaling the crisp air of a glorious Mount Athos morning, I felt as if I might burst. The air was laden with the scent of flowers, the birds were pouring out song, and the sleepiness I'd battled throughout much of the midnight services was replaced by a giddy elation.

It seemed only fitting, then, that we should enjoy a bit of wine with our breakfast.

As Nick and I filed behind the others into trápeza, I recognized modest carafes of white wine distributed among the bowls of garlicky potatoes and squid, the platters of olives and feta. I slipped onto my bench beaming. I poured out thanksgiving as the prayers were said and as the readings began. At the sound of the bell, I filled my steel cup with cool wine, and, catching Nick's eye, signaled a toast to his health, *stini yiassou!* I was slightly less enthused when— filling my mouth with a first, greedy draught—I realized I was drinking retsina—*bane* of Greek festivals across America, the one false move possible to make when ordering at a Greek restaurant. In my eight years among the life-savoring Greeks, I've developed a nearly fanatical taste for virtually all the pleasures of the Greek table—with this one notable exception. Retsina is—forgive me, belovéds—a sin against grapes.

I drank it just the same, and tried not to wince noticeably.

———

After trápeza, we rested in our room for an hour or so, and set off—gratefully without backpacks—for Moni Karakálou, a three-mile walk along an ancient, cobbled path through dense forest. When we emerged into a clearing an hour later, we were met by what looked to be a pristine medieval castle rising up from a surround of equally pristine monastic gardens—all of it poised atop a slope facing the turquoise calm of the sea. Within the gates we found a spotless, stone courtyard—distinctly unlike the patchy grass and packed dirt of Philothéou—surrounding the monastery's flawless sixteenth-century katholikón. Despite its age, Karakálou has the look of a monastery that was freshly painted yesterday, as if the monks here might be Swiss converts, or retired gardeners from Versailles.

Well, they are neither. The oldest are actually monks from Philothéou, who, years before, had come to a failing, decrepit Karakálou in hopes of restoring it to a thriving community. That's exactly what they did. I was now beginning to notice that the monks of Philothéou had been responsible for a good many such missionary activities in recent years, both on the Holy Mountain and abroad.

Once inside, Nick startled me by asking the gate master if there might be a priest available for confession. I hadn't so much as thought of such a thing, but for Greek nationals, apparently, confession with a *pnevmatikós*—a word that means spirit-bearer, and implies both confessor and spiritual doctor—is a staple of a pilgrimage to the Holy Mountain. When Nick's confession had been arranged, he asked the priest if there might be someone to hear my confession too, a pnevmatikós who spoke English.

I was relieved to learn that there was not.

Confession is an element of the ancient church that has remained difficult for me to embrace, despite my developing awareness of its necessity. That is to say, I understand how essential it is to admit to our failures, our sins, how helpful it is to receive counsel for avoiding similar failures in the future, and how sweetly the assurance of forgiveness works as a powerful and life-renewing gift. Still, though you can take the boy out from among the Baptists, it is something else to excise an embedded sense of Baptist individualism from that boy's dim wits—even if he would welcome the surgery. "Why," my inner-Baptist-child complains, "why do I need a priest for this? There is but one mediator between God and man," he says, thumping my heart, "and that is Jeeeeesus."

Amen.

Still, something subtle and necessary happens—and happens uniquely—in the sacrament of confession. Something that we need to let go of is finally relinquished when, and only when, we speak of our sins to another flesh-bound brother or sister—something that is not relinquished when we confess from the privacy of our closets. Self-protecting pride—the source of *all* sin—is given up, given away. That mask we each so carefully maintain in the presence of others is necessarily set aside, if only for a moment.

It is, brief as it is, a very humbling and a very freeing moment. That is to say that I have learned to appreciate the sacrament, but generally that appreciation is registered afterward, and seldom beforehand. Nick, on the other hand, had been looking forward to this opportunity all along; guilelessly, he had assumed I was similarly eager. The English-speaking pnevmatikós was not available, thank God. I let it go at that, though I spent the next hour or so staring out at the sea, grilling myself about my ambivalence while somewhere in a nearby chapel Nick fearlessly shed his pride, along with whatever other sins he'd hauled along.

When he returned—grinning ear to ear, in fact—we walked the tailored grounds as we waited for Vespers to begin.

———

I've never been to a Vespers service that didn't strike me as beautiful. The particular beauty of Psalm 103 is unfailingly heartbreaking. The sweetness of the vesperal melodies, the pathos of evening prayers that bring together thanksgiving, praise, and supplication—especially the earnest prayer for the salvation for all humankind—can melt a heart of ice. That said, the Vespers at Karakálou were the most lovely I had ever heard. Even Nick, who's been around the liturgical block a time or two, said the same.

We stayed at Karakálou for the evening meal of orzo and olives in a refectory alive with a peculiar evening light that made luminous the air itself, and also luminous the life-sized icons covering the length of all four walls and the ceiling. Then we strolled back the four miles to Philothéou, barely speaking a word.

I had been on the Holy Mountain a little more than twenty-four hours, but already a palpable calm was settling in. Along the way, I said the Jesus Prayer, modifying it to speak the names of my wife, daughter, and son at the end of each petition for mercy.

Crossing ourselves, we entered the monastery gate, and made our way to our small room. I lay down on the narrow bed and was asleep almost immediately, mid-prayer.

5

in remembrance of me.

Our second Divine Liturgy at Philothéou continues to haunt me.

Unlike the previous day, when muscle cramps and cold had kept me from resting well during the night, I woke from our second night on Athos with the first stuttering percussions of the tálanton, and I was immediately awake, as if cold water had been poured across my face. The air was crisp, the sound of the tálanton brisk and echoing in the hallway.

I hurried to dress in the dark. Not sure if Nick was intending to get to orthros and, given that his back had been hurting him, not sure he had been able to sleep well, I slipped out the door without waking him.

The air was even sharper out in the courtyard, but not as biting as the night before, nor as windy. I pushed open the huge wooden door and slipped into the narthex of the katholikón. Again, I stood for a moment just inside the door to get my bearings, allowing my eyes to adjust to the deep darkness. A single lit taper in the candle stand trembled in the rich well of the narthex, and in that faint light I could see that three or four monks were already settled into their stalls. I venerated the icons with greater care and with less self-consciousness than the day before, and entered the sanctuary to venerate the several icons inside. At the icon of the Theotokos, I paused to light a candle and felt someone right beside me reaching to do the same. It was Nick, grinning in the candlelight, whispering, *"Kalimera, philemou"*—"Good morning, my friend."

We found stalls in our familiar corner behind the left choir, and settled in to pray with the reader, who was just then beginning the psalms. Again, I was struck by the status of the psalms as prayer rather than as recitation. And here in the middle of the night, the luminosity of the reader's candlelit face—young and sparsely bearded—manifested a strange intensity mixed with softening adoration. Some moments later, a second reader arrived, taking his place at the stand in the center of the opposite choir, and then, as the hymns began—the *kathismáta*, *evlogitária*, odes, lauds—the two choirs continued filling with other *psalti* and other readers. Orthros continued with surreal beauty, and led directly into the doxology, which then led to the appalling announcement of the Divine Liturgy: Blesséd is the kingdom of the Father and the Son and the Holy Spirit, now and for evermore—words that join, ever and again, the visible body to the invisible body and its unending hymn.

On this day—perhaps because I was, as I say, slightly less self-conscious, slightly less stunned, slightly more able to follow along—the Divine Liturgy felt seamless, of a piece, and utterly gripping. I had a good sense of how those first emissaries to Byzantium felt, the ones who reported back to their Ukrainian Prince Vladimir: "We did not know if we were in heaven or on earth."

————

As the liturgy moved to conclusion with the Holy Mysteries—more beautiful, it seemed, than even the day before—I prepared to partake of Communion. Monday is generally a fasting day on Mount Athos, and, apparently, the resident monks will not receive Communion on fasting days. Therefore—I soon learned—if on a fasting day a pilgrim didn't make his way to the chalice as it was presented, the chalice would, most often, be immediately returned to the altar. Perhaps this sense of our having to hurry contributed to the horror of what then happened.

I was still peering from my stall, back behind the left choir with Nick, when I saw the first of the pilgrims moving toward the chalice uplifted in the priest's hands. I turned my head to make my way to the front when I heard shouting, something in Greek, loud, angry-sounding. It was the priest who was shouting, and quite sternly, to the man before the chalice. Nick told me later that the priest was saying, "Open your mouth." The surreal beauty of the liturgy turned immediately into surreal shock. I saw the priest raise the spoon to the pilgrim's lips, and then saw the priest's face go ashen with horror. And then he was shouting something else, not angry this time, but pleading. This time, says Nick, he was begging, "Don't move, hold still."

Immediately, two monks appeared at the pilgrim's sides, gripping his shoulders and holding him absolutely still, as the priest covered the chalice with the scarlet cloth and, without moving his feet, handed the chalice back through the royal doors to the deacon, who returned it to the altar. From the choirs, three other monks arrived with lit candles, moving in slow motion, inspecting the floor, the pilgrim's clothing, his shoes.

Somehow or other, the Holy Mysteries on the end of that spoon had fallen from the man's lips. And this is what I beheld: For the next half hour—during which time I barely breathed—the priest picked up every possible bit of the elements that he found on the pilgrim's clothes and shoes; he picked up every stray bit of *anything* he found on the marble floor, be it the Holy Mysteries or candle wax, lint, or speck of mud, and placed it in his mouth. The pilgrim was now openly weeping; one of the monks holding him relaxed one hand to pat his shoulder. When the priest was as certain as he could be that nothing remained on the floor, the trembling pilgrim was led through the left-hand deacon's door and back to the area around the table of oblation. Another monk arrived with a glass vessel, from which the priest poured an abundance of thick liquid. He then set a lit taper to the pool, and the entire marble floor before the royal doors came alive with blue flame.

When the flames burned away, the monks and pilgrims were called forward to venerate the icons, and to receive antídoron and a blessing from the priest's hand.

We then fled to the courtyard.

Unlike the day before, we all stood—monks and pilgrims alike—in awkward silence for what seemed a very long time. The bell sounded for trápeza, and, following the monks' lead, we filed through the refectory doors. Just before I entered, I turned back to look toward the katholikón, and saw the man who had spilled the Mysteries being escorted through the church doors by a young monk. The monk held one arm around the older man's shoulder, showing him a warm smile as well. The man's dress shirt was missing, and he seemed to be limping.

It took me a moment to notice that he was missing a shoe.

———

Spilling the Holy Mysteries—allowing the *very body* and *very blood* of Christ to fall to the floor—is not a commonplace. That said, the quickness of the monks' response and the surprising deftness with which they dealt with the event suggested to me that they had witnessed something of the sort before. The shirt, I learned, and, presumably, the shoe were to be burned; the man was treated with care and genuine warmth, and led to trápeza by a solicitous monk.

I ate my potatoes and olives quickly, barely tasting them. Something of the fear I'd apprehended the previous day returned and nibbled at my thought, accompanied by a vague, if passing, sense of dread. If there had been wine—even retsina—I would have drained my cup in a single draught. I studied the orange in my hand without eating it, and when we'd been released, I received the blessing of the abbot, and hurried with Nick to the gate for our ride to Karyés.

We'd been told that a ride would be along immediately after trápeza. It would be a taxi service supplied by one of the Athonite monks; so, when we found a Land Rover warming up in front of the gate with a monk behind the wheel, we assumed it was for us.

Nick asked the monk if he was going to Karyés. The monk said he was, so we got in, even though he seemed a little surprised that we did. I sat in the passenger seat while Nick hopped in back. Shrugging, the monk began to drive, but only drove a few yards before stopping again; though the monk kept rubbing at the windshield with the back of his hand, it kept fogging up in the cold. Glancing at the dashboard controls, I saw that, given their settings, we'd be there until mid-May before that window cleared up any. I offered one of my few Greek words, *signómi* (excuse me), and reached to fiddle with the controls; the windows cleared immediately. The monk beamed at me, saying, "*Doxa to Theo*," and we tore off, with surprising speed, which I took to be incentive to recommence the prayer in silence.

After a very few minutes, Nick struck up a conversation with the monk in Greek, and in so doing learned that he wasn't the taxi monk at all. He was, instead, the monastery's representative to the governing body at Karyés, having been called to meet regarding the helicopter tragedy of two days before.

After a few moments of awkward silence, we were all laughing as Nick explained the misunderstanding, and we zipped down the dirt road toward Karyés.

———

The father dropped us at a fork in the road so we might have a closer look at the expansive ruins of Saint Andrew's Skete before heading into town. Though it is a "skete," Saint Andrew's is much larger than many of the ruling monasteries, covering about fifty acres. It was abandoned during the aftermath of the Bolshevik Revolution, fell into disrepair, and suffered extensive fire damage in 1958. Then, in 1992, a Father Pávlos and a handful of monks—*again*, from Philothéou—settled there and set to work, restoring the katholikón and many of the buildings. They have accomplished a great deal in relatively little time. The katholikón was locked, but, from the outside, it appeared to be huge.

We could have stayed the night at the skete, and met with the monks who had settled there, but I was eager to extend my diamonitírion to the full ten days I had counted on; and we were both eager to get to Grigoríou and Simonópetra, where we hoped to make contact with two monks whose names we'd been given by my friends Chris Merrill and Nicholas Samaras. So Nick and I headed into town for a little paperwork before we caught the dusty bus to Dáfni.

Near the Prótaton, at the administrative offices of the monastic republic, we found the man to do the deed—a small and slightly officious man in a brown uniform—but when Nick asked him to add six days to my permit, he frowned and said, according to Nick, "That's too long. No." Even I understood his stern "*ohi*." Then he spun on his heels and disappeared through one of several doorways leading to a honeycomb of offices.

Nick looked perplexed, and I took all of this to mean that I would have to rethink my plans, and try to make the most of what little time I was given. We sat for a while, strolled around the entry hall, checked the clock to see that we wouldn't miss the bus back to Dáfni, and about fifteen minutes later the official returned, handing me my diamonitírion. I looked at the dates he'd filled in, and saw that he'd granted me the full ten days anyway. I blurted out, *Ne, ne, efharistó!* (yes, yes, thank you!), and he nodded, finally meeting my eyes; he asked if I was Greek. When I said, *"Ohi, ime Scotzézos-Americanós,"* he asked, smiling now and nodding, if my mother was perhaps Greek. I said, *"Signómi, ohi. Ine Anglída-Americanída."* His smile evaporated. He shrugged, and wished us both good health, shrugged again, and went back through a side door, returning to his hidden offices.

We scrambled down the steps, stuck our heads in the door of Dimitri's shop to say our good-byes, then hurried to catch the bus to port. We hadn't been able to secure rooms at Simonópetra, but had arranged two nights at Grigoríou before Nick would catch the boat back to Ouranoúpoli; he had business to attend to in Athens—including arrangements to have our parish's Gospel book bound in silver and gold. After Nick had gone, I'd be on my own for six days.

The bus dropped us in Dáfni with about an hour to wait for our boat, the *Ágia Ánna*, during which time I had further opportunity to pilgrim-watch. I also had plenty of time to consider why I had come here in the first place, and to entertain an array of second thoughts.

Though I had come to find a spiritual father who could assist me in prayer—counsel me in my increasing desire for a life of prayer—most of my energy had, so far, gone into dealing with logistics and culture shock. The journey had been intermittently strenuous, disturbing, and beautiful—and I had found that since my arrival the prayer was very often on my lips—but I had some doubt that I would find what I had come for.

For one thing, I had yet to meet a monk who spoke English; and I was realizing that my Greek was just barely good enough to order breakfast, or to annoy a local official.

Our boat ride from Dáfni to Grigoríou was so brief that our arrival caught us a little by surprise. As the ferry was making the turn into the cove protecting the *arsanás* of Moni Grigoríou, Nick and I scurried to the lower deck; we found a good-sized crowd of pilgrims waiting there

to disembark, as well as a crew of men preparing to carry off what looked
to be a mixed load of goods: bushels of leafy produce, sacks of potatoes,
more heavy bags of concrete mix, bundled lengths of rusty rebar.

We all crowded into the lower hall of the archondaríki, where
we found a table loaded with customary guest tray fare: cold water,
loukoúmi, Greek coffee, and *rakí* (a Greek version of grappa, also known
as *tsípouro*), which offers—it turns out—a refreshing, late-morning
jolt. We were met (I wouldn't say exactly welcomed) by an exceedingly
stern-faced monk barking what sounded like a much-practiced litany
of instructions, none of which contained any words I recognized.
This monk—I would learn much later—was Father Damaskínos, an
estimable polyglot, inexhaustible dry wit, and accomplished writer.
He is also—when he's not herding pilgrims like cattle at Grigoríou—a
missionary to the Congo, where he has labored for many years serving
the agricultural and spiritual development of the region.

When he had finished his cranky litany, I took courage to approach
him, asking in elementary Greek if he, perhaps, spoke English and
could translate some of what he'd just said. His face tightened; he
gave me a quick look up and down, shook his head, and walked away
without a word.

Eventually, we were given a room to share with a couple other men,
and when we'd stowed our packs, Nick and I hit the trail to Simonópetra.
Our plan was to see what we could of the cliff-top monastery—though
we'd been told there was "no room in the inn"—and to make contact
with Father Iákovos, a monk that my friend Nicholas Samaras had
insisted we meet.

Simonópetra—all seven stories of it—is perhaps the single most dramatic edifice on the Holy Mountain, poised as it is on the very tip of "Saint Simon's Rock," an outcropping of granite rising more than a thousand feet above the sea.

—— *Another View of Simonópetra* ——

The downside was that we would have to hike up to it. The trail begins steeply enough, but at the end of the hour-long trek, it gains— I'm guessing—nearly a thousand vertical feet in about as many steps. Long story short: we were aching and, once again, dripping wet when we entered the small courtyard beneath the archondaríki.

We found water in a stone fountain there, and inhaled a liter or two; then we slipped into the shadows to pull off our sopping T-shirts and slip into dry ones. At the top of the wooden stairs leading to the guestmaster's post, we met a young monk who welcomed us and gave us seats on the balcony overlooking the sea; he brought us loukoúmi, water, and rakí. As he was setting off to boil coffee, we asked him if Father Iákovos was available. He blinked in surprise, but said he would check.

We were well rested and relatively cooled down by the time Father Iákovos climbed the guesthouse steps to meet us. A relatively small man with a manifestly sweet spirit, his smile and piercing eyes lit up as he welcomed us, embraced us warmly, and asked where we were from. Something about his immediate interest in us made me uncharacteristically shy for much of this first visit. His concern for us was humbling; he tried unsuccessfully to secure us a place for the night, asked the names (and the name days!) of our wives and children, and encouraged us to come back when there might be room for us to stay. He gave us a tour of the katholikón, where repairs following a recent fire were nearly complete, and then he led us to Vespers in a small chapel deep in the rock upon which the monastery is built. Then he led us to trápeza for the afternoon meal, and thereafter escorted us to the veneration of the relics, where he whispered to us an English translation of the presiding priest's Greek explanations of each.

This was my first experience with the veneration of relics, and I was keen to understand. Over the past eight years, I had come to understand *something* of the Orthodox reverence for the dead—that is, for those we call "the beloved departed." A great many of the subtleties of Orthodox faith—its not-exactly-Western appreciations of the body, of beauty, of Communion, of the immediacy of the kingdom of God, and of the life-giving Presence of the Holy Spirit—are figured, embraced, and practically demonstrated in this uncommon reverence. Once, in fact, when I had glimpsed how such reverence for the dead is inextricably connected to an abiding faith in the Resurrection, I pursued the matter further in a poem that had, at the time, surprised even me.

Here's how it ends:

> . . . *Every altar in our churches bears*
> *a holy fragment—bit of bone most often—*
> *as testament to the uncommon and genuine*
> *honor in which we hold the body—even*
> *shattered bits of it, even when its habitant has,*
> *for all appearances, gone hence. Each mute relic*
> *serves as token both of death and of life's appalling*
>
> *ubiquity—even there. It helps to bear in mind*
> *the curious and irreparable harm the Crucified*
> *inflicted upon the nether realm when graved*
> *He filled it with Himself, and in so doing, burst*
> *its meager hold and burst its hold on us—all*
> *of which has made the memory of death lately*
> *less grim. Gehenna is empty, and tenders*
>
> *these days an empty threat. Remember that.*

Well, I *was* remembering a good bit of that as I listened to Father Iákovos. The narrow table before the Royal Doors held a large piece of the True Cross in a cruciform reliquary of silver, relics of Saint Anne, the mother of the Theotokos, of Saint Panteleímon, of Saint Tryphon, the skull of Saint Sergius, the right hand of Saint Dionysios, and the left hand of Saint Mary Magdalene—which held, even then, a surprise for me.

I crossed myself and brought my lips to the small oval opening where the back of her hand was visible in its silver reliquary. I kissed

Magdalene's hand—the right side of my mouth meeting the cold metal and the left side of my mouth pressing against the hand itself. And then I startled to the abrupt contrast between the cold metal and her quite warm hand, and startled to the sense that this hand, removed from a bone box in the first century, was not only warm, but tender as living flesh.

Make what you will of that.

I take it as a token of life's appalling ubiquity. And even now, writing about this months later, I still feel the warmth of her hand on my lips.

At Father Iákovos's encouragement, I passed my prayer rope to the priest so that he might bless it with the relics of the saints.

—

As I say, it was my friend, the poet Nicholas Samaras, who had insisted we get to Simonópetra to meet Father Iákovos. The two of them had been in seminary together; and as we visited with Father Iákovos, we discovered that he had also been in school with our priest back home, Father Dean. He had also been there with Father Joseph, a kind and tireless priest from St. Louis, who had traveled regularly to serve our community before Father Dean arrived; and they had all been in seminary with the chancellor of our diocese, Father Dimitri.

Big faith, small world.

Before we headed down the trail again to Grigoríou for the night, Father Iákovos led us to the cave where the monastery's founder, Saint Simon, had lived for many years as a hermit prior to the series of visions that would lead to his founding the monastery and establishing the community there in the thirteenth century. Nowadays, a small chapel is set in the cliff face, protecting the cave; but the cave opening itself is little more than a chink in the granite, rising some four or five feet and opening to a small void of roughly four feet high, five feet wide, and maybe seven feet deep. This is where Saint Simon Myroblite—the Myrrh-Gusher—entered the kingdom of God, even in the midst of life.

In other words, this is the very spot on earth where a living Saint Simon became prayer.

The Chapel Protecting Saint Simon's Cave

As we prepared to hike back down the trail to Grigoríou, Father Iákovos asked again about our wives and our children; he wanted to remember their names, as well as our names, in his prayers.

We embraced—his eyes were like bright black coals—said our good-byes, and clambered down the dusty trail in silence to Moni Grigoríou on the shore.

There are two guest areas at Grigoríou, a lower guesthouse near the pier and a second wing of rooms within the walls of the monastery itself, poised about a hundred yards uphill. For our first night, Nick and I had been given beds in the lower house. Down here, we would not hear the tálanton, so I set my travel alarm for 3:00 AM, and fell asleep saying the prayer. It seemed like no time at all before the alarm sounded, and as I lay there aching and weary from three days of Athonite life, I wondered if I could maybe sleep in today, arrive a little later in the services.

None of the other men was moving—a couple were still snoring— so my conscience wasn't nagging me too terribly as I closed my eyes and dozed off again. That, evidently, was all it took to fully rouse that very conscience, which then poked me pretty hard. I woke again in seconds, and nearly suffered whiplash as I sat up, feeling that I had left something important undone. As I sat in darkness on the edge of the bed, I took a couple deep breaths, and said my morning prayers under my breath as I dressed.

I pretty much ran up the stone steps of the mule path and into the interior of the monastery; I slipped into the narthex just as the reader began the hours.

The katholikón at Grigoríou is slightly smaller than that of Philothéou. It is also slightly less dark. I found my spot—what was becoming my habitual spot—in a narrow *stasídthi* immediately behind the left-hand choir, then settled in to pray. Within moments, I was lapsing in and out of the same, weird, waking-dream state that would confront me intermittently. I was also beginning to feel the throb of a caffeine-withdrawal headache. Let this be a lesson to us all, especially to caffeine addicts like myself: dose yourself in increments along the way, or you will surely pay. In time, I learned to fill one of my water bottles with a cool mix of Nescafe, which I sucked up whenever the telltale ache began in the tender fuse box at the top of my spine. Cold instant coffee. Desperate measures for desperate times.

But back to church.

A young novice was being taught to chant, and his discomfort was evident. He gripped the readers' stand as if it might run off, and kept adjusting the oil lamp overhead as if more light might help him find the pitch. He was well below the pitch most of the way through, and struggled to find an approximate melody to suit the tone of the day. In Orthodoxy, there are eight liturgical tones—with certain, ethnically inflected variations—in which the services are sung. Most Orthodox services are, for the most part, sung or intoned throughout. For the preliturgy hymns, in particular, the tone changes every week, and this week we were enjoying tone one, even if this morning none of us was so far exactly enjoying it.

By the time we made it to orthros, other *psaltes* had arrived, mitigating the ordeal for the young novice, as well as the ordeal of our hearing him. The young man stayed at the stand, but was happy to sing under his breath, trying to memorize the complex riffs of Byzantine chant, tone one.

Nick arrived at the beginning of orthros, and slowly the katholikón filled with other pilgrims. At one point, I looked around, wondering where most of the monks had gone.

The Divine Liturgy was beautiful, as always. When I went to partake of the Holy Mysteries, I stood before the cup, said my name, Isaák, opened my mouth, and closed my eyes.

Nothing happened.

I opened my eyes to find the priest studying me as he held the spoon firmly in the chalice. Quietly, he asked, "*Íste Orthódoxos?*" ("Are you Orthodox?"). I stammered, "*Ne, ne, íme! Íme Orthódoxos, Orthódoxos Americanós.*" He nodded, raised the golden spoon, saying, "The servant of God Isaák receives the Holy Mysteries."

I crossed myself, received antídoron from a platter on the readers' stand, and slipped back to my corner stall.

———

In the courtyard, after breakfast (our breakfast wine this morning was red, and quite tasty), Nick and I asked some of the monks if Father Cosmás was around. A friend of mine, the poet Christopher Merrill, had struck up a friendship with Father Cosmás, a monk from England, during his previous visits to the Holy Mountain, visits that were for him a time of healing—following his time reporting on the Balkan Wars—and about which he has written a beautiful book. Chris had encouraged us to seek out Father Cosmás, who'd been the guestmaster during Chris's various stays at Grigoríou, and was now—we learned— the host of the upper archondaríki. When he'd been pointed out to us, we pretty much cornered him in the courtyard outside the trápeza; he seemed happy to be caught.

6

freely you have received

Father Cosmás is, I'm guessing, a man in his early forties—late thirties, maybe; his ready, smiling hospitality and casual manner make him seem, intermittently, much younger. His British accent also seemed something of an incongruity here on this Greek peninsula, if one that seemed less so as my time on Mount Athos led me to perhaps a half a dozen men from Australia, one from New Zealand, and several other Brits.

He invited us to the kitchen for coffee, and we spent the rest of the morning there at the kitchen table, swapping stories, until Nick headed down the hill to meet the first of the two boats that would take him back to Ouranoúpoli. At one point, Father Damaskínos—the somewhat stern host of the lower archondaríki—came in to fix a pot of tea. He looked my way and said, "*Bonjour*," almost smiling. When his tea was ready, he poured his cup and turned to go, calling out, "*Guten tag!*"

Throughout the total of four days and nights I would spend at Grigoríou during this first trip, I would never get a single word of English out of Father Damaskínos—though I was told he was fairly fluent. He greeted me each time we passed, but always in a different language—French, German, Dutch, Italian, and one or more African dialects. He didn't smile much, but I could see he was enjoying himself.

———

Father Cosmás arranged for me to move to the upper guesthouse, where he served as host, and we were therefore able to visit off and on throughout that day and the following morning. He has the calm demeanor of a man who has found his place, has found his home here amid the rigors of monastic life. I asked him where I should visit for the remainder of my stay, and he suggested that I backtrack to Karyés and use the microbus to get to Megístis Lávras—Great Lavra—then hike along the base of the mountain at the southern edge of the peninsula. That way, he said, I could get a good sense of the environs of the most ascetic of the Athonite monks, the hermits of Vigla (the area around Lavra and Timíou Prodrómou Skíti at the peninsula's southeastern tip) and of Katoumákia (between Kafsokalivíon Skete and Saint Anne's Skete at the southwestern tip).

So, that was the plan. Before I set off to meet the boat to Dáfni, however, I took courage to speak to Father Cosmás about my reasons for coming to Athos. I told him about my relatively faltering prayer life, and my desire to find a holy man to guide me.

He seemed surprised, then evidently moved. "This is a very good desire, Isaák," he said. Then, as we sat over our mugs of American-style drip coffee, he said that he didn't know of any such men living on Mount Athos now.

I was floored, and must have shown it, because he hurried to say, "Don't misunderstand, there are *many* holy monks here, many wise and holy men, but those who have the gifts you're after are not likely to be found."

I was slightly less floored, but still a little puzzled. "What do you mean?" I asked him. "They're not here at all, or they're not where I'd find them?"

His eyes met mine with what I took to be compassion, and he said, "I just don't know where to send you."

———

This was not such good news. I puzzled for a moment about the many ways such a statement might be meant, but kept my puzzlement to myself. I saw that it was time to set off. Father Cosmás offered to keep some of my things—books, gifts for home, extra clothes—so I wouldn't need to haul them in my increasingly heavy pack. He also asked to borrow my copy of Saint Isaak of Syria's "second part," a collection of homilies that had only recently been recovered and translated into English. At that point, the book hadn't yet been translated into Greek. With that offer,

Father Cosmás also made sure that I'd be stopping in again at Grigoríou before heading home. I asked him to put my name on the guest list for my last two nights on Mount Athos, and headed to the pier.

———

The routine was much the same as before. Board the boat, cruise to Dáfni, grab a *spanikópita* and a coffee at the patio café, then shove my way onto the bus for Karyés. This time, when I hit the parking lot, I sought out the microbus for Great Lavra, and piled in with a good many others. The microbus—a Mercedes—had seating for twelve, but we had managed to squeeze sixteen men inside. The driver surely would have fit more inside if there had been other takers. He had personalized the dashboard area with all manner of saints' cards, prayer ropes, crosses (woven, carved, or stamped out in varicolored plastic), and seemed to be saying something under his breath throughout most of the nearly two-hour drive to Lavra. It wasn't until we were nearly there that I leaned in to hear what he was saying—*Kyrie Iisou Hriste, eléison imás*, a short form of the Jesus Prayer.

———

Great Lavra is, well, quite frankly, *great*; it is immense. In Orthodox tradition, there are, essentially, three modes of monastic life. Eremites—the hermits—of course, live for the most part in solitude; a small groups of monks might compose a skete; larger groups compose monasteries. The largest monasteries are sometimes called Lavras. That said, you might gather from its very name that *Megístis Lávras* is one big, big monastery. You would be correct.

Besides officially being the oldest among today's twenty monasteries—the "ruling monasteries"—it is also first in the traditional hierarchy of those communities. It is genuinely huge, spreading out across an area roughly the size of, I'd guess, about a dozen football fields, resembling a medieval village more than a single monastery. Much of it has been restored, much of it is in the midst of restoration, and great stretches of it remain in dire need of repair.

We were dropped off in the parking lot, and followed the signs (finally, signs!) to the archondaríki, where we signed in, and enjoyed the usual welcome of cold water, loukoúmi, rakí, and Greek coffee (pretty much received in that order) while we awaited our room assignments. Of the fifty or so pilgrims arriving, nearly all were Greek, the exceptions being me, a man from the Ukraine, and two Japanese, one of whom was, quite surprisingly, a Zen monk in a saffron robe.

Receive this however you will. It took about an hour for the majority of the rooms to be doled out, during which time we all waited in the archondaríki and in the guest patio. Two by two, the Greek men among us were installed in rooms with two or three beds. Once they'd all been assigned rooms, we four—two non-Greek Orthodox and two Japanese disciples of Zen—sat in the courtyard awkwardly awaiting our assignments; we tried conversation, without much luck; then, we waited for another hour or so. Finally, the guestmaster happened by, seemed surprised to see us still there, then, shrugging, waved for us to follow him.

He led us to something of a barracks, a cavernous room holding about thirty beds, and motioned for us to settle in. One thing I hadn't fully gathered until this point was how some monasteries—not *all*, mind you, but some—take pains to keep non-Orthodox "visitors" from mixing with the Orthodox "pilgrims."

Many monasteries restrict non-Orthodox to the narthex during services. Some set separate tables for them during meals, or, in extreme cases, feed them afterward or in adjacent rooms. Some, it turns out, also assign them to separate sleeping quarters. In this case, the monks at Lavra were careful to do pretty much all of the above. One unique twist, however, was that the Ukrainian and the American were also considered non-Orthodox—or, perhaps, not quite Orthodox enough. Or something. The Ukrainian was visibly annoyed. I was perversely entertained. The two Japanese men took it in stride, and offered me some dried apricots and cashews.

I spent the afternoon poking around the enormity of Great Lavra alone, picking my way through one dusty courtyard after another, discovering chapel after chapel, workman after workman, monk after

—— *Great Lavra* ——

monk. Most of the day was punctuated by the sounds of drilling, sawing, and hammering; I wondered how the monks managed to pray amid such wall-to-wall cacophony. Even after three hours of traipsing the grounds, I never did manage to get my mind around its rolling expanse. Those grounds include—by rough count—something like half a dozen large churches and thirty-five chapels; the central katholikón dates from AD 963. From what I could gather, more than three hundred monks live there, having relatively recently returned to a coenobitic rule. The trápeza—whose ceiling is supported these days by an imposing network of steel scaffolding—is immense, its tables and benches carved out of marble and granite, with room for, I'd guess, more than a thousand men.

Up the slope and away from the sea, some two or so miles above Megístis Lávras—roughly a third of the way to the summit of Athos itself—lies a very notable cave. These days, it is part of a monastic enclave of several kéllia. It is the place where a fourteenth-century monk acquired a life of prayer that would lead to a very important turn of events later in his life, when he would serve as bishop of Thessaloniki and defend "the prayer of the heart" from scholastic critics, unduly influenced by the West.

Hesychasm, in general, dates back well before the twelfth century, but its most articulate defender was Saint Gregory Palamás, the monk of that Mount Athos cave. *Hesychía* (*eh see KEE ya*), the condition toward which the hesychast strives, is often translated as "silence," but I think we do better with "stillness," as that stillness suggests a condition of the whole physiology and psychology, not just the vocal chords.

It is a stillness that occasions, as well, an actual healing—a re-*pairing*—of mind and body, what some would call a "*noetic* regeneration." The *nous*—that noun from which the adjective, *noetic*, springs—is a word found throughout the Greek New Testament and throughout the writings of the Fathers and Mothers of the Church. In translation, its import is almost invariably lost.

Most often rendered as "mind" or "reason" or "intellect," these poor translations are complicit in our unfortunate dichotomy of the human person into a two-part invention: a relatively deplorable vehicle (the body) and its somewhat more laudable passenger (the spirit). Along with an insidious doctrine of secret, saving knowledge given to those whose spirits have transcended bodily bondage, this very dichotomy is, frankly, such a dire misunderstanding as to constitute its own species of heresy, namely Gnosticism. You might recognize its legacy as an ongoing, body-bashing error among a good bit of the Western Church, both high and low.

A clearer understanding of the *nous*, therefore, would be a very good thing—and it is one good thing to which I hope, somewhere along the journey, to attend.

But where was I? Wandering in the woods beneath Saint Gregory's cave, recalling his story.

———

As most of us one day discover, the greatest hindrances to spiritual maturity, spiritual equilibrium, and wholeness are the countless distractions that keep the head turning to and fro, keep the mind flitting from one fragmentary blip to another, and keep the body more or less twitching in response—not to mention the heart racing along as if pursued. This composite "white noise" keeps our brains buzzing, and our persons dissipated.

Abba Nicephoros the Solitary puts it like so: "Let us return to ourselves . . . , for it is impossible for us to become reconciled and united with God, if we do not first return to ourselves, tearing ourselves—what a wonder it is!—from the whirl of the world with its multitudinous vain cares, and striving constantly to keep our attention on the kingdom of God, which is within us."

Saint Isaak of Syria says, "Descend into your heart, and there you will find the ladder by which you may ascend."

The hesychasts are canny about the chaos, and they seek control over that whirl of circumstance by developing a habit of stillness, of *watchfulness*, which avails a consequent habit of apprehending God's Presence, and—as I like to say—*leaning wholly into It*.

En route to this sweet apprehension, they observe their own, scattered faculties being gathered, restored, reunited—being knit back into a seamless self. Thereupon, they apprehend a re-union of that self with the Holy One as well.

Or so they say.

Or so I've read, and so I'm pleased to believe.

———

Theology, as you already may have noticed, comes in two broadly popular flavors: the more familiar *kataphatic* (the theology of attributes, the *via positiva*) and the somewhat less familiar *apophatic* (the theology of negation, the *via negativa*). At its intermittent best, the West has understood the two approaches as equal and largely complementary, each approach balancing the other. In the Western model, for instance, one might say—*kataphatically*—that God is King, which would reveal something of God's relation to us; but one would hasten to—*apophatically*—balance that assertion by insisting God is not King the way a man would be king. This hedging of the term would eventually yield to an understanding that God is, finally, in no way comparable to a king, or to anything else—being God and all, and inexhaustible.

In Eastern Christendom, the apophatic is understood as the higher approach outright, a fuller, more appropriate perception that grows out of what is often an initiating, kataphatic glimpse. In the midst of apophatic apprehension, one would watch each of the familiar, kataphatic metaphors—*king, father, judge,* for instance—fail and fall away, revealing a glimpse of appalling enormity far beyond *any* of the gestures by which we attempt to define God.

I like how Saint Gregory of Nyssa puts it after he puzzles and pores over the Exodus passage regarding how Moses enters the darkness and finds God within it: "The true knowledge and true vision of what we seek consists precisely in this—in not seeing, for what we seek transcends knowledge, and is everywhere cut off from us by the darkness of incomprehensibility."

Simone Weil offers a very likely account of this apophatic vision when she writes:

A case of contradictories, both of them true. There is a God. There is no God. Where is the problem? I am quite sure that there is a God in the sense that I am sure my love is no illusion. I am quite sure there is no God, in the sense that I am sure there is nothing which resembles what I can conceive when I say that word.

To be fair, all theology—all "God talk"—bears at least a trace of both flavors. I'm pretty sure that most actual theologians, pressed on the point, would concede that all of their assertions about God come down, at best, to being words about what has been revealed by Him rather than words defining Him.

And the reason that all of these folks, confronted by the impossibility of defining God, don't just shut up about it—and possibly the reason that even Simone Weil, for all her genuine, hard-won humility, didn't just keep her disturbing thoughts to herself—is that we are none of us in this for ourselves alone.

Our selves, alone is finally a very undesirable circumstance, perhaps even a profoundly satanic circumstance.

For Saint Gregory Palamás, the issue came down to how we might acknowledge, on the one hand, God's absolute *beyond-us-ness*, and, on the other hand, God's condescending love for us, and union with us, as revealed by His apparent desire that we partake of His Holy Being.

Saint Gregory Palamás spoke, therefore, of a difference between presuming to know God in His *essence* and our coming to know God in His *energies*. We cannot—not ever, according both to Saint Gregory Palamás and to long-standing Orthodox conversation—hope to know God in His essence, but we can know *of* Him in His energies. We can witness His works, His acts, His effects; moreover, we can experience them, experientially *know* them. Such knowledge enables—one might say that such knowledge *animates*—our faltering faith, just as participating in, partaking of, those divine energies animates our faltering life.

Saint Gregory Palamás and the other holy hesychasts of Mount Athos lived by these energies, which by habits of contemplative prayer they came more fully to apprehend and to appreciate. By these habits of prayer, they understood that humankind was created in order to (again, my favorite figure for this) *lean into* those energies, dwelling, as it were, *on* them and *in* them.

My guess is that—inveterate *choosers* that we are—we are forever leaning one way or another. Choosing to lean *into* the Holy Presence is to taste, here and now, of the kingdom of God; choosing to lean *away* is to taste, here and now, hell.

The monks of Mount Athos lived deliberately by these energies in the twelfth century and long before; they live by them today, as do we, if not so consciously or deliberately. Not all of the monks on Mount Athos—nor all of the monasteries there—pursue an absolutely hesychast tradition, but all do cultivate elements of that tradition, in particular the constant awareness of God's Presence, and the desire that our lives become prayer.

This, then, is the significance of *lives of prayer*, a significance I'm beginning to better understand as I go along. Such lives are lives *composed of* prayer. As the Orthodox theologian Paul Evdokimov puts it: "It is not enough to say prayers; one must become, be prayer, prayer incarnate. It is not enough to have moments of praise; all of life, each act, every gesture, even the smile of the human face, must become a hymn of adoration, an offering, a prayer. One should offer not what one has, but what one is."

————

In my long afternoon of meandering around the grounds, inside and outside the great wall of the Great Lavra, I never heard the tálanton, but at around four in the afternoon I barely made out the bell calling us to Vespers; I followed that sound to the central katholikón. The Vespers service was, not surprisingly, lovely—a sweet conclusion to a busy day. The antiquity of Great Lavra is quite palpable; as I prayed I apprehended an uncommon weight here, as if this oldest of the twenty monasteries bore, even in its air, a corresponding, accumulated heft. At the conclusion of Vespers, I walked to the courtyard in what felt like a numbing, ethereal fog; I languished there for a half hour or so, until the bílo called us in to eat our potatoes and beans.

————

As I've mentioned, the Holy Mountain has a curious effect on pilgrims, seeming to bring out the best in some, and what looks to be the worst in others. It is fair to say that it brought out both in me, in reliable sequence. At trápeza, one pilgrim—a guy about my age, if slightly grayer, certainly more dour—seemed to take it upon himself to be captain of the piety police.

During meals—as I've mentioned—the general convention is silence. Men file in, take their places as directed by the monks, stand until the prayers of blessing are completed, then sit on wooden benches or stone slabs, and dig in. No one is supposed to speak; all are expected to listen carefully to the words of the appointed reader—who, for the most part, is reading excerpts from the lives of the saints, albeit in Greek. Still, on occasion, a pilgrim or two will ask for bread to be passed, or will reach to pour water and offer to fill the cups of those around him; in other words, quietly and reverently a few words and gestures are sometimes exchanged without much fuss.

For the self-appointed sheriff at our table, however, this casual behavior was not to be condoned; it was to be corrected, and without delay. If a man reached for the water pitcher too soon (one convention is to wait for water until a few minutes into the reading, when a small bell jingles, signaling "drink up"), or if someone made a comment to a neighbor, our sheriff manically gestured for silence. The young man next to me—twenty-ish and pleasant—asked me to pass the bread. The sheriff, sitting opposite us, hissed. The young man gave me a quick look and smiled, raising an eyebrow. The sheriff glowered at us both. The young man took a bite of his orzo and said, "hmmm." The sheriff put his finger to his lips and shooshed him.

A moment later, the young man reached to the end of the table for the bowl of olives, and the sheriff slapped his hand.

These perplexities pretty much dominated my thoughts as I settled in to sleep that night in our huge barracks. The isolation of the Japanese men, the nearly identical isolation of the Ukrainian and myself, the pious ass at dinner (along with the not exactly unique disposition he came to represent for me) had me feeling a little lost, had me wondering what I was doing here.

———

When the tálanton woke us at 3:00 AM, I dressed in the dark and hurried to the katholikón, where I found Sohsen, the Zen monk, already sitting—by which I do mean *sitting*, Zen style—in the narthex. This is as far as he would be allowed to enter, but he sat calmly, eyes closed, breathing his silent meditation in that presence-laden space.

The service was, as expected, beautiful. Still, though it wasn't a fasting day, the Eucharist was presented and returned to the altar before anyone (either monk or pilgrim) had opportunity to partake—yet another perplexity of life at Great Lavra. We filed from the katholikón directly into trápeza, where, once again, I was seated directly across from the sheriff. I smiled when our eyes met, and he turned away, scowling. The young man from the night before sat at an adjacent table and, when he'd caught my eye, smiled, and gave me a thumbs-up, nodding to the sheriff. The meal went passably. There was no wine. I managed to break my fast without incident, and without—so far as I know—giving further offense to my tablemate.

After trápeza, I packed my gear, studied the map, and set my sights on Saint Anna's Skete, a six hours' hike to the west. This day's trek would take me through some of the most isolated territory on the Holy Mountain, a region where the most strenuous ascesis was pursued by the most rugged of spiritual athletes.

First, however, I would need to find the trail out of Great Lavra's expanse, ideally heading in the right direction. Most of the other pilgrims rushed to the microbus immediately following trápeza, but in the courtyard, I found a thirtysomething man talking on the card phone.

When he had hung up, I asked, in pretty poor Greek, if he knew where the trail to Saint Anna's Skete started. He said—in English that was only slightly better than my Greek—that he was going that way as far as Skíti Timíou Prodrómou, the Romanian skete.

Along the way, I learned that he was on liberty (either that or his name was Liberty, Lefthéros?) from the Greek Army, and that he was here to spend time with his spiritual father, a hermit named Father Pávlo, who lived near the Romanian skete. Lefthéros, I learned, visited this spiritual father at least four times each year; he had been to Athos fourteen times over the previous three years.

We walked together quietly, savoring the coolness of the morning and attending to a forest alive with birdsong and powerfully fragrant pine. In about an hour, we turned off the road and onto a trail leading toward the shore and to the gates of the lovely skete, which we entered crossing ourselves. Though it is a skete, Timíou Prodrómou appears slightly larger than some of the smaller monasteries, and similarly structured—a fortified wall of stone buildings circling a central katholikón. The fathers there are mostly Romanian, and their welcome was quite warm. Lefthéros and I enjoyed our rakí, loukoúmi, and cold water, and—once we were refreshed—were invited to venerate the icons in the *kyriakón*, the skete's main church.

———— *The Romanian Skete of Saint John the Forerunner* ————

It was one of the sweetest, most lovely churches I'd yet seen. We lit candles, venerated the icons, and were able to stand praying for a good and peaceful quarter of an hour before the monk who'd let us in said he had to get back to the archondaríki.

Back on the trail, Lefthéros shook my hand, pointed the way I was to go, and calling out, "*Iássou, phílemou!*" headed down the slope toward the shore, where his Father Pávlo awaited him.

I tried not to be jealous.

—— *"The Desert" of Karoulía* ——

7

a reed, shaken by the wind . . .

Alone again, I grinned to discover that much of the ambivalence haunting me during my time at not-so-Great Lavra had dissipated—due, no doubt, to the immediate kindness of Lefthéros, our warm welcome at Timíou Prodrómou, and the lush quiet of the skete's kyriakón. I actually started singing as I hiked, growling out a sequence of Greek hymns from the Divine Liturgy.

I had walked a good hour or so when I stopped to fill my water bottle from a plastic spigot spliced into a black water hose that ran along much of the trail. As I sat cooling off, I noticed some twenty yards down the shaded trail a blue plastic bag—like a grocery bag—tied to a branch. At first, I assumed some pilgrim or other had dropped it—there *had* been a surprising bit of litter along the trail—but then I noticed the bowl at the base of the tree, a Tupperware bowl with a lid, no less. The blue bag—it appeared—was meant to call attention to the bowl.

This, I gathered, was how some hermits survived here at the farthest end of the peninsula, an area where there are no roads, few trails, and where even the ferry boats cannot land; this is what the Athonites refer to as *the desert*, and this bowl was how one such hermit procured food to supplement the wild greens he gathered to boil for his food.

I dug into my pack to pull out the bag holding the last of my trail mix, and left it in the bowl. As I continued down the path, I called out "*Evlogeíte!*" If anyone answered, I didn't hear him.

About an hour later, I came across a similar bowl at the base of another tree. I didn't think I had anything to leave, but then remembered the jar of peanut butter at the bottom of my gear.

Slipping the pack to the ground, I turned to see a man approaching from the direction of Lavra. It was Sohsen, the Zen monk, walking in sandals, carrying only a staff and small cloth satchel slung over one shoulder. He waved, smiling as he approached, then took my hand to shake it when he got close, saying, "Good to meet you now, Isaak." I offered him water from my bottle, and we sat for a moment together, cooling off. Then I dropped the peanut butter jar into the bowl, swung up my pack, said *iássou* to Sohsen, and headed off. Over the course of the next three or so hours, we met just about each time one of us stopped to rest; we shared water, apricots, and several comic attempts at conversation.

Alone again, with Sohsen somewhere behind me, I was pretty worn out when the path began a steep downward slope; turning into the first descending switchback, I saw the sea—the southern end of the Holy Mountain's western shore, and saw, well down the slope between me and the sea, what looked to be a hillside village—*Skíti Ágia Ánnis*, Saint Anna's Skete.

I was even more worn out and dripping wet when, after a full hour of switchbacks in a steep, knee-popping descent, I wobbled through the entry gate to the small courtyard between the kyriakón and archondaríki. In one corner, under the shade of a simple wooden gazebo overlooking the sea, a group of men sat sipping rakí and coffee; one of them was a monk, who looked to be about my age. They all turned to wave hello as I dropped my pack and began to dig into it for a dry shirt. The monk called out something in Greek, to which I called back, "*Signómi, then milaó pollá Eleniká!*" He must have caught the accent, for he called back, "Plenty of time to change later! You won't offend us! We're not offendable. Come refresh yourself!"

That sounded like very good advice. I leaned my pack against the stone wall and joined the men in the shade. The monk asked, "So, my good man, do you have a reservation for the night?"

When I told him I hadn't, he said, "Well, in that case, you'll have to be punished. Sit down and take your punishment." He slid the tray of rakí to where I could reach it.

There were, all told, eight of us sitting around the table—the monk, whom I will call Father Seraphim, six Greek men from Thessaloníki, and I. We visited with Father Seraphim for much of the afternoon;

he switched readily from Greek to English as needed, and over the course of our visit told me that he had grown up in Seattle, that he was researching and writing a history of Orthodoxy in America, and that he, too, had gone to seminary with my friend, Nicholas Samaras, as well as Father Iákovos, Father Dean, Father Joseph, and Father Dimítri. Much later, during the return boatride of my third trip, I learned that at this meeting Father Seraphim was also the *dikaios* of the skete, the community's elected leader. While the abbots of monasteries are elected for life, the dikaios of a skete is elected annually by the older monks of the community.

At one point, he turned to me and asked directly—and, apparently, out of the blue—"Who is your spiritual father?"

This cut me to the quick. I'm sure that my face must have shown something of my surprise and my puzzlement. The demands of hiking strange and difficult terrain, the many mixed feelings I'd felt in response to the pilgrims and monks at Lavra, and the nagging (and increasing) sense that I was on a wild goose chase had all left me—at least for the moment—distracted from my purpose in coming here in the first place—which was to *find* a spiritual father.

I wish that I had been ready to say something like "Funny you should ask. I'm actually trying to find him."

Instead, I stammered something like "I confess to my priest," to which he smiled and slid me a second shot of rakí. Within moments, it occurred to me that my answer may have sounded slightly militant to Father Seraphim; there has been, after all, in some circles a long-standing tension between those bishops and priests who serve parishes and those monastics who honor the tradition of the elder, the *staretz*, the *yéronda* (*YEH ron da*). Something of this tension is articulated as early as Dostoevsky's *The Brothers Karamazov*, where a good number of the local priests (and certain of the monks themselves) manifest resentment toward the devotion that the local folk show to Father Zósima, who also serves as their confessor. I would have made certain Father Seraphim hadn't misunderstood me, but there wasn't time; someone else had arrived. Sohsen was at the gate.

The looks on the faces of the other men nearly made me inhale my rakí. As it was, my eyes teared up as I tried to keep from laughing, and tried to keep the burning liquor from rising up and out my sinuses. They could hardly believe their eyes.

Sohsen leaned his waking staff near my backpack and walked toward us beaming. Father Seraphim stood to greet him, and as he did Sohsen brought his hands together in reverence and bowed low. Then he reached to kiss Father Seraphim's hand.

The men were stunned, and Father Seraphim was visibly moved by the gesture. He responded by saying, in English, "Welcome," and by kissing Sohsen on both cheeks.

"Come," he said, gesturing to the group, "join our little gathering, brother."

Sohsen joined us at the table, and we all settled in to enjoy coffee and sweets.

Off and on, during our visit, another tray of sweets or coffee would arrive. We were all pleased to be served—except, perhaps, for Sohsen, who, as the cups were drained, gathered them onto a tray, and slipped into the kitchen to wash them.

Father Seraphim watched him with great interest, and apparent admiration.

At one point, one of the Greeks—a retired restaurateur who, I gathered, was staying at the skete all summer and helping in the guesthouse kitchen—brought out a cupboard door he wanted to resize for a new cabinet. He laid it flat on the table under the gazebo and commenced to saw it. Rather, he commenced to saw *at* it, trying to remove a strip of about three inches from along the length of one side. He wasn't doing very well, and a couple pilgrims sidled over to help him. They, too, had a hard time making much headway through the hard chestnut panel.

From where he sat, Sohsen was studying the situation, with what looked like a trace of a smile. He didn't move at once, but watched closely. In turn, each of the three men struggled with the saw, sweating profusely, making little progress, then setting the saw down for the next man to try. As soon as the third man relaxed his grip on the saw, Sohsen was standing beside him gently taking the saw from his hand. In a flash, he had stepped atop the table and was standing right on top of the door. He braced himself and began sawing. The saw went through the length of the board like butter. It took him about a minute and a half to finish the job.

When we were given rooms, once again, Sohsen and I were put together. This time, however—in stark contrast to the barracks of Great Lavra—we were put in a beautiful little room with two beds, a writing desk, and a heartbreaking view of the southern slope of the skete—as well as the peak of the Holy Mountain itself to the left, and the blue Aegean to the right.

———

There was no general Vespers service here; Saint Anna's Skete remains an idiorrythmic community, and the fathers customarily observe Vespers in one of the chapels or in their cells. Even so, after trápeza we were all escorted—Sohsen included—into the church to venerate the icons and the relics there. Prominent among the icons is a wonder-working icon of Saint Anna holding the infant Theotokos; the icon's golden frame is lined with dozens of photographs of young children and newborns. Father Theóphilos, companion to Father Seraphim and the monk who seemed to be the primary guestmaster, told me in English that these photographs were sent by men and women who had previously been unable to have children. As it turns out, this is one of the skete's primary missions to the outside world; from here, the monks send a small box of blessed items—a length of ribbon, a vessel of holy water, a vial of chrism, and square bits of antídoron—to any couple who asks for them. They also send along a booklet of prayers and instructions for fasting, taking the water and the antídoron, and using the ribbon and the chrism before attempting to conceive. The monks also pray before the wonder-working icon for the couple's fruitfulness.

The photographs were astonishing—dozens of lovely children lining a beautiful icon of our Holy Mother held by her holy mother. "That's a lot of children," I said to Father Theóphilos.

"These are just the photos for this month," he said.

We then moved to a narrow table that Father Theóphilos had set before the Royal Doors of the iconostasis, and watched as, one by one, he brought out an array of relics, reverently placing them on the table's scarlet cloth.

Saint Anna's Skete was actually founded, sometime around 1689, to preserve one of these very relics—the left foot of Saint Anna, the mother of the Theotokos. This relic remains central among the many protected at the skete, and I must admit that a curious sweetness, a warming of the heart, attended my veneration of it. From the moment I had arrived at Saint Anna's, I had felt something of this sweetness. I had attributed the sensation to finally being able to sit down after a long and grueling hike, and to the warm welcome I'd received from Father Seraphim. I had even thought that the aesthetic power of the place—it *is*, after all, absolutely beautiful—made me imagine a particularly sweet presence there. When I kissed the relic—which, incidentally, smelled strongly of heady spice—all other explanations were replaced by a powerful sense that Saint Anna herself sweetened the entire place.

Don't worry; I don't expect you to believe me.

Then again, it hardly matters.

Suffice it to say that, on this first trip, Saint Anna's Skete proved to be one of my favorite spots; I planned to return. One cannot fail to sense the deep peace of God's presence there. And Saint Anna, whose life had, previously, registered only slightly in my thinking, has become a saint to whom I daily speak.

The evening concluded with our visiting quietly in the broad alcove and patio between the guesthouse and the church. The monks had disappeared, the pilgrims had become, for the most part, introspective, and the evening settled in like a cool garment over us as we watched the sun disappear into the deepening blue of the Aegean. The peace was something you could touch, breathe in, taste, and see.

———

I woke at around 3:00 AM, to see that Sohsen had already gone out. I said my prayers and headed to the chapel for the midnight hours. This was my first experience of liturgy in one of the small chapels on the Holy Mountain. These chapels are, for the most part, where most monks celebrate the Divine Liturgy on most days. There are exceptions (the monks at Simonópetra being a *notable* exception), but the monks of certain monasteries begin the midnight services in the central katholikón, only to disperse toward the end of orthros to continue the liturgy itself in these small, intimate chapels, where a handful of monks—sometimes as few as two—celebrate the Eucharist.

This morning, about six pilgrims gathered at the cemetery chapel with about the same number of monks. One chanter and one priest led the service simply, quietly, and at a lovingly attended pace. The reading, the chanting, the censing, all took on a notably sweet and intimate quality there in the roughly two hundred square feet of the nave and narthex. I had found a stall in the back left corner of the nave, and I could have stood there forever.

As midnight prayers blended into the orthros, and then into the Divine Liturgy, I said the Jesus Prayer under my breath, more alert than ever to the powerful sweetness I felt here at Saint Anna's. Off and on, I noticed I was weeping, not sure why—no sobbing, no choking up, just a steady flow of tears down my face, wetting my beard. The uncommon beauty of worship—the intimate closeness, the frankincense, the simple chanting, the sense that I was part of a centuries-long prayer —became an apprehensible ache in my chest.

During the cherubic hymn (the slow hymn that attends the "Great Entrance," the procession of the elements for the Eucharist), I sang along softly in Greek, and during the litany that followed, I noticed Father Theóphilos studying me from his stall near the psalti stand. I worried for a moment that I shouldn't have joined in singing the hymn, or that I hadn't sung softly enough . . . or something. I worried that I had made *some* kind of faux pas that caught the monk's attention. I was wrong.

As the litany concluded, and as the psalti intoned the *Father, Son, and Holy Spirit*, Father Theóphilos crossed directly over to me and set a hand on my arm; into my ear he whispered in English, "The Symbol of the Faith, do you know it?"

"The Creed?"

"Yes, the Creed. Do you know it?"

"Yes, I know it," I whispered back.

"Very good. You say it now, in English please!"

I didn't have time to defer. We'd come—that very second—to the place in the liturgy when the Creed is recited. Panicked, and fearful that I'd forget something, I spoke out, as firmly as I could, attending to the words as, perhaps, I had never done before.

When I had finished, Father Theóphilos patted my arm, beaming. "Yes," was all he said. He returned to his place near the psalti as the liturgy continued. When time came for the recitation of the Lord's Prayer, once again, Father Theóphilos was at my side, asking me to recite the prayer in English.

Being asked to recite these two moments of the Divine Liturgy is, by the way, a special honor given to visitors—most often to visiting priests. That Father Theóphilos decided to offer this honor to an English-speaking pilgrim is itself a symbol of the uniquely welcoming spirit of Saint Anna's Skete.

I received the Holy Mysteries that morning feeling giddy. After the service, we filed out and met up under the gazebo for coffee. I kept hoping Father Seraphim might show up in the guest area before I left. He didn't, and I kept wincing at the thought of having missed what seemed to be my best chance yet to find a confessor, and a spiritual father.

I did, however, have a warm and helpful conversation—over biscotti and coffee—with Father Theóphilos, mostly regarding the miracle-working icon, and how folks went about requesting prayers for conceiving children. I kept thinking that my own children may find the information useful somewhere down the line.

And, later on, as I started off on the trail toward *Moni Agiou Pávlou* (the Monastery of Saint Paul), I kept turning around in the path for yet another glimpse of the heartbreakingly lovely *Skíti Ágias Ánnis*, which is, even now, fixed in my heart as a uniquely sweet, powerfully holy place set upon an entire mountain of sweet and holy places. I had hoped, as well, to catch a final glimpse of Father Seraphim.

8

I have called you friends.

Along the way to Saint Paul's, the trail cut into the ridge above *Néa Skíti*, New Skete—which is more formally, if seldom, called The Skete of the Nativity of the Theotokos, indicating a strong connection to Saint Anna, as well. While Saint Anna's Skete— just a mile or so to the south—is a dependency of Great Lavra, New Skete is a dependency of Saint Paul's. Like Saint Anna's, New Skete is idiorrythmic, and though I didn't stop there on this first pilgrimage, I was struck by the beauty of its expanse, its chapels and kéllia spread out across a steep, forested slope reaching to the sea.

For half a mile or so, I shared the trail with about a dozen mules that seemed to enjoy staying just ahead of me, snagging mouthfuls of greenery as they sauntered along.

At a second fork leading down to New Skete, they took the low road back and left me to finish the morning hike alone.

The hike to Saint Paul's from New Skete was almost completely along a level path, a welcome break from the steep descent that had sorely tested my knees at the end of my hike the day before. The weather was also slightly cooler, so when I arrived a couple hours later in the broad canyon holding Saint Paul's, I was still relatively fresh, and eager to explore the rugged terrain there. This late in the summer, the "river" that once formed the canyon is little more than a stream; judging, however, from the breadth of the river bed—and by the enormous boulders that compose and surround it—I had a good sense that the springtime runoff here must be quite a sight.

The footpath led onto the midpoint of the broad road of crushed granite that connects the monastery to its *arsanás*, its port; I hiked up that road and to the bridge over the river. The monastery itself is well protected, its ancient walls built into the granite of the slope. There are,

actually, two protective walls here—one outer ring protecting scattered
kéllia, workshops, and storage sheds, and an older, more daunting
ring, protecting the traditional, inner sanctum around the central
katholikón. Between these two, just above the gardens and vineyards,
a relatively modern guest quarters occupies one broad terrace with
a commanding view of the canyon, its extensive monastery gardens,
and the sea poised between two steep and rugged points. Just outside
the inner gate, a large square gazebo overlooks the scene as well. As I
approached it, I met an old monk also approaching, but coming from
the monastery gate; he, too, was apparently a visitor. Like a good many
of the very old monks, he was very small—even childlike in stature.
He nodded to me as he caught my eye, and I approached him, saying,
"*Evlogeíte.*"

"*O Kyrios,*" he said, smiling, giving me his hand.

As I kissed the hand, he blessed me, and asked my name.

"Isaák," I said. "Íme Isaák."

He smiled broadly and asked, "Isaák o Syros?"

"Ne, Pater, Isaák o Syros."

"Kalá! Kalá!" he said beaming.

Though he is relatively unknown among American Christians
in general, and only slightly better known among American
Orthodox, Saint Isaak of Syria, my name-saint, is famous on the
Holy Mountain and in monastic communities around the world.
His *Ascetical Homilies*—written, for the most part, to offer practical
help and spiritual guidance to monks—are widely read and revered.
He has helped countless monks in their struggle toward lives of
prayer, and he has helped a good many other, slower pilgrims along
the way as well.

The old monk and I climbed the few steps to the gazebo platform
and settled in, dropping our packs to await the guestmaster.

It turned out to be a pretty long wait.

One disadvantage to hiking from monastery to monastery—
as opposed to using the boats and ubiquitous microbuses—is that
guestmasters tend not to notice your arrival. These days, most pilgrims

—— *Saint Paul's Monastery* ——

prefer the buses and boats, so most guestmasters tend to plan their activities around the schedules of these transports.

Fortunately, the gazebo was comfortable, shady, and cool, and the view was stunning. I took the opportunity to settle into prayer. The old monk was way ahead of me, his prayer rope already being drawn, knot by knot, between his fingers.

A couple hours later, I was roused from that stillness by the sight of the boat—the *Ágia Ánna*—gliding into view. About half an hour after that, the microbus pulled up to the gate with its load of pilgrims; that's when the guestmaster hurried out from the gate to herd us all inside and upstairs to the archondaríki to sign in.

Here again, at Saint Paul's, I realized that my status as not-exactly-Greek translated into my being not-exactly-Orthodox. The guestmaster put the others—about twenty, all told—into small rooms in groups of threes or fours, and assigned me, by myself, to a huge room with roughly twenty bunk beds. At this point in my journey, I was beginning to puzzle over the wide disparities between communities like Simonópetra, Grigoríou, and Saint Anna's—where the stranger is warmly embraced—and communities like Great Lavra and Saint Paul's—where the stranger seemed more likely to be kept at arms' length. I went out on the terrace to think it over.

That's when Yórgos—one of the pilgrims I'd met as we'd all signed the guest book—strolled out of the guest house and came over to visit.

Yórgos was there with a group of friends—Stamátis, Evángelos, and Nicholas—accountants from Thessaloníki, all of them in their late twenties or early thirties. This was an annual trip for most of them. The others came out soon thereafter, and after Yórgos had introduced us they offered me cigarettes and cold coffee. I was happy to get the coffee. After about five minutes, I was no longer Isaák to them; they called me *Sákko*.

Their English was, for the most part, pretty good, and we were able to cobble together a friendly conversation, sharing photos of wives and children, generally enjoying the afternoon together.

At one point, we walked down the slope to a domed shrine about midway between the arsanás and the monastery. This shrine marked the spot where, in 1457, the gifts of the Magi had been presented to the fathers here. Tradition has it that Maro, the stepmother of Muhammad the Conqueror, had come to "return" these relics to the Christians, and though she had been one of the very few women—at the time—to have set foot on the Holy Mountain, this spot, maybe a quarter mile from the sea, was as far as she'd dared to go.

We entered the open-air shrine, opened the glass-paned doors of the icon shelf, and relit the oil lamp inside. One by one, we venerated the icons. Our prayers were brief and silent, but the very fact of our praying together simply, unselfconsciously, was a refreshing contrast to the more familiar spectacle of public prayer back home.

———

The tálanton called us to Vespers soon after we returned to the guesthouse terrace, and we hurried into the gate to the church. The central katholikón at Saint Paul's is very like katholika elsewhere on the mountain, except that a wide, glassed-in exonarthex—itself lined with beautiful icons—serves as entry from the stone courtyard.

The day ended much the way it had ended for me throughout much of this first pilgrimage: Vespers, trápeza, and an evening walk. When night fell, filling the sky with stars and one very round moon, I left my fellow travelers out on the terrace, and hiked back down the cobble path to the shrine. I was feeling a little melancholy. I would, after all, be leaving the Holy Mountain in about three days' time, and my plans of finding a spiritual father on the Holy Mountain now appeared pretty foolish, and very unlikely.

At the shrine, I lit a taper, knelt before the icon of the Theotokos, and asked if she would please help me to know why I had come here. To the Christ in her arms I said, "Lead me to someone who will help me find the prayer of the heart."

I made my way back up the path, slipped into the solitude of my vault of a barracks to say my evening rule—leaning against one wall and facing, roughly, the east. Then I lay down and closed my eyes, continuing the Jesus Prayer in the dark, struggling harder than usual to attend to the words, to dwell upon them. Certain faces were playing back in my memory—the priest at Philothéou, his eyes glowing with candlelight as he brought the golden spoon to my mouth, the bright and loving eyes of Father Iákovos, the deadpan jests of Father Damaskínos, the hand-clapping laughter of Father Cosmás, and the easy warmth of Fathers Seraphim and Theóphilos. My melancholy and second-guessing persisted, pretty much until, quite suddenly, something in me calmed, and, presumably, I fell asleep.

———

I was again one of the first pilgrims into the services. I had come to prefer to arrive well before the others—even before many of the monks, as it often happened—so that I could venerate the icons, light my three candles, and breathe the prayer in the quiet of the nave unhurried. I also liked being able to find my habitual corner stall, or one near to it, so I could settle into prayer as the readings from the psalms began.

This day, the service *flew* by—which is maybe a curious thing to say about *anything* that happens over the course of four hours. Still, the rhythm of worship, the rhythm of prayer, and, to some extent, even the rhythm of life on Athos was becoming—had become—familiar and satisfying. The long services had begun to feel less like an endurance test and more like the one continuous prayer it is intended to be.

As is often the case, liturgy was followed by trápeza, which was followed by our packing up and preparing to leave. As I did, I startled to realize that I hadn't so much as spoken to a single monk who lived here. I'd spoken to the yéronda—the old monk—in the gazebo as he, too, awaited the guestmaster; I'd also spoken for a few minutes with another friendly visitor, a monk from Australia; but none of the resident monks had made themselves available to the pilgrims, even after Vespers and trápeza, when a few generally will make such an effort.

The immediate friendship offered by Yórgos, Stamátis, and the others had distracted me from so much as noticing this before now. I went out with my backpack, and found my friends smoking on the terrace; they offered me coffee, cold and sweet. The weather had darkened a little, with a thick curtain of rain clouds being drawn across the horizon; from what I gathered of their conversation, Stamátis and some others would be joining me to walk to Dionysíou—just over an hour's hike up the coast—while Yórgos and Evángelos would take the boat some hours later.

We said our good-byes, and Yórgos especially wished me well, saying he hoped we'd meet again at Dionysíou or sometime in Thessaloníki. We embraced, exchanged the traditional two-cheek kiss of the Greeks, and headed down to the trailhead near the beach. He shook my hand firmly, met my eyes, and he said, "*Kalo taxidi, Sákko.* Good the journey."

Good the journey. Exactly.

——

The hike from Saint Paul's to Dionysíou—which is nearly identical to the hike from Dionysíou to Grigoríou—is a series of steep ascents seaward, rising to briefly level stretches atop and around sun-drenched headlands overlooking the Aegean, followed by steep descents away from the sea and into narrow canyons—green, shaded, smelling of fresh water and damp earth. The trail transects four or more such headlands before descending into the significantly wider canyon holding the monastery.

Our little group huffed and puffed during the ascents, we caught our breaths through the level stretches, and we joked and laughed during the brisk descents. The accountants from Thessaloníki proved to be very good company, and it was with real regret that I left them at Dionysíou. I could have stayed the night, but I was eager to get back to Grigoríou, where I could bend the ear of Father Cosmás. I stopped just long enough to enjoy my last guest tray with my crew, then headed out for the next ascent. Halfway up that first stretch of trail, I heard a distant, echoing "Sakko-o-o-o," shouted from the direction of the monastery. Squinting, I could make out a bunch of what looked to be accountants from Thessaloníki, waving their arms from a high porch near the top of the monastery's sheer wall.

——— *Dionysíou Monastery* ———

As the trail took me up the first ridge and down the other side, I focused on the prayer. I'd be spending my last two Athos nights at Grigoríou, and with only a few days left, I was anxious to firmly establish the prayer before returning home—something of a grim irony, really, being anxious to attain stillness.

Fair to say, this last hike of my first journey became one long and earnest prayer—a prayer for prayer. I had all but given up on finding a father.

——— *Return trail to Moni Grigoríou* ———

The sight of Moni Grigoríou from the final ridge gave me a surprising sense of homecoming. Its stone walls and slate domes, perched atop a sheer cliff rising from the sea, were softened by a late-morning haze. The trail led in a series of switchbacks descending through olive groves, and brought me to the cemetery plot and its lovely chapel. As I passed the chapel, striding toward the monastery's back gate, I walked beside a large tin bucket resting on the chapel steps. It held two dark brown femurs, an amber skull, and several broken bits of bone.

Not knowing exactly how to respond to my strange discovery, I crossed myself and nodded in respect, then hurried to the back gate.

———

Father Cosmás was serving coffee to new arrivals from the boat when I showed up at the archondaríki. Carrying a large silver tray laden with a good twenty cups of muddy residue, he flashed his famous smile, and nodded for me to slip directly into the kitchen—rather, into the small dining room off the kitchen where he and I had visited earlier in the week.

When I did, I found that Father Cosmás had another guest as well. Robin Amis, a writer-scholar from England, was sitting at the table, working on a laptop computer identical to my own; several open books and manuscripts were spread out across the table before him. He looked up over the top of his glasses, and said, "Ah, an American."

I confessed, and introduced myself.

Robin—a regular visitor to Grigoríou—was visiting this time to assist Father Cosmás with a new translation of *The Deification as the Purpose of Man's Life*, a book on théosis by Archimandrite George, the abbot of Grigoríou. Abbot George is a prolific and much-respected theological writer. His books include studies of experiential grace, the Lord's Prayer, théosis, and other matters of spiritual growth.

———

I believe that I have mentioned already that everything about life on Mount Athos is best understood as a means to an end.

Théosis, it so happens, *is* that very end. It is—one should take care to notice—an end that turns out to be endless.

Discipline, obedience, fasting, even putting up with pilgrims— every aspect of ascetic struggle on Athos—is understood to assist in humility, which is understood to assist in prayer; and prayer—a life that has *become* prayer—is understood as the central, indispensable path to théosis. It is, in short, the experiential translation of humanity from death into life.

Or, it might be said to be the gradual realization of the existential translation from death to life that Christ has brought about.

Already.

That is, even the long and difficult path to a life of prayer is understood to be a means of glimpsing, taking part in, *living into* a reality that—thank God—is already so.

Saint Athanasios writes famously and provocatively that "God became man, so that man might become god." For those Western Christians who might find this equation bordering upon heresy (an impression that, for Eastern Christians, poses something of a comic irony), you might bear in mind that God is forever unknowable, never to be equaled, much less eclipsed—which is to insist that every incremental development toward deification that a man or woman apprehends will concurrently avail, for that man or woman, a fuller and truer vision of God's inexhaustibility. That is, the more we become *like* God, the more powerfully we appreciate how far beyond our prior understanding He—endlessly—*is*.

I think I already mentioned *Enormity* as a likely figure.

Let's go with *inexhaustible Enormity*.

That said, the human person who, through théosis, becomes like God, does so via the death-defying agency of Christ, in whose Divine Life that man or woman participates. By His death, we say, "Christ has undone Death." By His incarnation, we are grafted onto His divine life.

The Deification as the Purpose of Man's Life is a very good and savory book, but Father Cosmás, Robin Amis, and—most significantly— the abbot himself have been somewhat dissatisfied with an earlier translation into English. Their new translation seeks to make available to English readers some of the subtleties and powerful implications that readers of Greek already enjoy.

Nous, as I've noted already, is a word that has often suffered from translation, being reduced simply to "mind," or "reason," or, slightly better, "intellect." The new translation will not translate *nous* into any of these—will not translate it at all—but will endeavor to introduce the complexities of the word itself, and will endeavor to introduce the *noetic faculty* to a broader array of English-speaking Christians.

To quote the glossary notes Father Cosmás shared with me:

———

The nous is our highest faculty. It has been called the "eye of the soul," the "eye of the heart," and also the "energy of the soul" by various church fathers. Since the fall, and the [consequent] fragmentation of the soul, the nous may identify itself with mind, imagination, or the senses, losing sight of its pure state. When cleansed, the nous is able to perceive itself, perceive God, and rightly perceive creation; it is cognitive, visionary, and intuitive. Metropolitan of Nafpaktos Hierotheos has said, "The nous is in the image of God. And as much as God is light, the nous too has light mirrored in it by the Grace of God."

———

Bishop Kállistos Ware has called it "the intellective aptitude of the heart."

In most English translations of his Gospel, Saint Luke says of the resurrected Christ along the road to Emmaus, "Then he opened their *minds* that they might understand the scriptures." In the Greek of his original text, the word Saint Luke employs here is *nous*.

Virtually every time we come across Saint Paul's discourses on *mind*, his word of choice is *nous*; most notably, when Saint Paul writes about the sinful capacities of humankind, he observes that "since they did not think it worthwhile to retain the knowledge of God, he gave them over to a depraved *mind*, to do what ought not to be done." The word for that depraved faculty is also *nous*.

The *nous*, therefore, can either be whole or fractured, soiled or cleansed, availing either insight or delusion, depending on its condition.

Therefore, as the monks on Mount Athos struggle to see, feel, think, and imagine clearly and truly, they seek to do so by means of a grace-illumined, graced-restored *nous*.

———

So, we talked a good bit—Robin, Father Cosmás, and I—during these last few days of my first pilgrimage. My roommates for these two nights were two Italian Catholics, Paolo and Osvaldo. This was Paolo's first visit to the Holy Mountain, but it was Osvaldo's fourth. Curious about Osvaldo's interest in Athos, I asked him—with the help of Paolo, whose English was pretty good—what brought him here so many times. He said, according to Paolo, "God love."

Nice answer.

We hung out together, comparing journeys as we could. They took to calling me Zacco.

As Catholics, Paolo and Osvaldo were not, according to convention, allowed to worship in the nave itself, but were expected to worship in the narthex. I knew this, and, ostensibly, so did they. So, it was with an anxious-making tremor of surprise that—at the culmination of my last Divine Liturgy at Grigoríou—I looked up from prayer to see Osvaldo in line to receive the Holy Mysteries.

I wasn't sure what would happen, but followed behind to join the line as well.

What happened was this: Osvaldo approached the chalice, leaned forward, and opened his mouth. The priest lifted the spoon bearing the Mysteries, and said—roughly translated—"the servant of God. . . ." And he paused, waiting for *this* servant of God to say his name, whereupon the priest expected to continue, repeating that name and announcing "receives the Holy Mysteries."

Osvaldo's silence extended the pause. And the priest asked quietly (as he had one time asked me), "Iste Orthódoxos?"

Osvaldo said no, he was Catholic.

The priest said, "Signómi," shaking his head. He put the golden spoon back into the chalice, and made a sign of blessing across Osvaldo's brow.

This was actually a kinder response than it could have been, and I was relieved that so little fuss was made. Still, the look on Osvaldo's face as he turned and left the nave uncommuned made me wince. He looked heartbroken.

I received the Mysteries myself—also having to answer the pop quiz along the way, but doing so successfully—and turned to retrieve a piece of antídoron from the plate on the reader's stand. Antídoron is the remaining bread from the blessed loaf of leavened bread that is used for Communion; a small square—the Lamb—is removed and

—— *The Katholikón of Grigoríou* ——

consecrated for the Holy Mysteries, and what remains is then cut into small pieces for communicants to receive following their partaking of the cup.

I lifted a piece and placed it in my mouth. I took another, and cupped it in my hand. About ten minutes later, I found Osvaldo in our room, packing his things. He looked as though he had been crying. I took his hand, and set the small square of bread in it. He kissed me on both cheeks, saying, "Thank you, Zacco," the only English I had yet heard him speak. He stood facing the icon in the room, and placed the antídoron in his mouth, eyes closed. I left him to his prayers.

Grigoríou proved to be a very good last stop. Father Cosmás—by his genuine warmth, his genuine interest, and his serious questions as well as a fairly nonstop supply of hot tea—helped me, over the course of these final few days, to articulate the growing conflict that was complicating my impressions of the Holy Mountain.

Would I find a spiritual father, a confessor, a spiritual guide? Would I find him here on the Holy Mountain? In Arizona? Was I kidding myself?

At the very least, Father Cosmás was able to let me know that I was not alone.

As we parted in the courtyard after trápeza that Sunday morning, Father Cosmás loaded me up with copies of the abbot's books, some incense for my wife, and a small wooden icon of the Theotokos for our home. He also returned my copy of Saint Isaak of Syria's "second part," asking if I might send him a copy when I had the chance.

At the pier, I saw that there were about six of us waiting for the boat, including Paolo and Osvaldo. The boat was running late, so we all milled about, strolling back and forth across the concrete landing over the course of half an hour.

Once as I was strolling past Paolo for the umpteenth time, he offered a bit of Italian-inflected English; when he was just passing by my ear, he said, "Hello, meester."

On the boat, Osvaldo brought me a coffee, and one more kiss on the cheek.

PART TWO

THE FAR
AND
THE NEAR

9

without a parable, spake he not unto them.

I was glad to get home, glad to be back with my wife, our daughter Liz and our son Ben, especially glad to get home in time for my daughter's nineteenth birthday, which also marked the sixth anniversary of my oily welcome—my chrismation—into Orthodoxy, my embracing the fullness of the faith.

I was very happy, as well, to be greeted by Mona (my dog and my conscience), whose yelps of joy at my arrival home contained, I'd say, a soupçon of indignation at my having been gone so long. We now have *three* huge Labradors—Mona, and two of her onetime pups, Rita and Leo, who these days weigh in at 95 pounds and 110 pounds, respectively. All three dogs are huge, and any homecoming—whether it's after an hour away or thirty days—is also something of a bruising gauntlet.

I was also just beginning a year's leave from teaching at Missouri, so I settled into a routine of reading and writing, visiting and revisiting novels, poems, and a wide array of writings from early Fathers and Mothers of the Church. I kept to my morning and evening rule of prayer, and wore a prayer rope on my wrist to help remind me to continue the Jesus Prayer during the day.

Mostly, I worked on poems and prayer.

Increasingly, I've suspected and have tried to articulate a relationship between poetry and prayer—a relationship, even, between what I think of as genuinely poetic language and sacrament. Part of my failure, so far, has to do with my sense that the comparison has often led to sentimental reductions of both.

For starters, for about a decade now, I've been trying to come to terms with what it is that distinguishes poetry from the other genres.

The attempt has, itself, been instructive, mostly because this attitude of *coming to terms*—approaching words attentively, patiently, and without predetermination—is precisely the disposition required for anything approaching success in making a poem.

Among my students—among even the brightest of them—many start out by supposing that poetry is a species of denotative art, a laboriously embroidered species of that genus perhaps, but a primarily expressive, referential undertaking. Most imagine that the role of the poet is to express her unique feelings, or to share his comprehensive and world-correcting understandings. Some few still imagine that their job is to seek out vivid experiences they can then document.

My sense of actual poetry writing is that, before it can so much as begin, it must be recognized as *a way* by which we concurrently construct and discern experience; it is not a means by which we transmit ideas or narrative events we think we already understand, but a way we might discover more sustaining versions of them.

Like most endeavors of the spirit, poetry itself is a pilgrim's journey. We gather our gear, and we start out—alert to where the path will lead.

———

So, back home again, I worked on new poems, I puzzled over poetic texts, I fussed over what makes a poem a poem, and I continued in my pursuit of prayer. I also made plans for a return visit to Mount Athos during the winter, when, presumably, there would be fewer pilgrims and, maybe, a greater opportunity to visit with the fathers there. In particular, I wanted to spend more time with Father Iákovos at Simonópetra, Father Seraphim at Saint Anna's Skete, and, of course, with my friend Father Cosmás at Grigoríou. I wrote to each of these fathers, asking if they might pass along to their respective guestmasters my request for lodging.

———

On the morning of December 7, I was once again aboard the *Áxion Estín* with a boatload—a far lighter load this time around—of monks, pilgrims, and day laborers en route to the Holy Mountain. The wind was brisk and, off and on, rain-bearing as I stood on the deck, scribbling notes as the boat bounded, rocking and plowing toward Dáfni. As we thrummed along, the occasional scarf of dark cloud passed overhead, so quickly as to appear like a time-lapse film, dropping fat drops of rain before disappearing over the Athonite ridge. Off to the west, a broader, darker band of cloud hung brooding. Through scattered sections of that cloud, thick shafts of golden sunlight angled to the sea. Gulls were wheeling in every direction—affecting wheels within wheels, here between the heavenly city and the Holy Mountain.

Dáfni looked all but deserted as we rocked to the pier, but a good fifty or sixty of us clamored over the iron gangway onto shore. I grabbed a coffee—*ena Nescafe me gala, para kallo*—in the café and waited to board the *Ágia Ánna*, which would take me to the arsanás at Grigoríou.

As I sat, sipping the piping hot coffee, I noticed a few familiar faces. For one, the tall Bulgarian monk I'd first noticed—months earlier—scraping a lottery ticket in Thessaloniki was here again, standing alone at the seawall and looking out at the rain clouds, the shafts of sunlight; he didn't have a lottery ticket this time, but was instead thumbing the knots of a *chótki*, a prayer rope.

The entire demeanor of the place had softened correspondingly, having slowed down a good bit. Frankly, it seemed more like what I'd imagined it would be during the months preceding my first trip. The crowds were gone, and with them the harried pace, the short tempers, and most of the shoving.

When the crew of the *Ágia Ánna* lowered the gangway for the dozen or so of us boarding the boat, we strolled aboard slowly, and the crewman selling tickets was actually polite, smiling as he yawned.

———

A total of four of us disembarked at Grigoríou—compared to about fifty who did so in September. I wasn't planning to stay the night—I was on my way to Simonópetra—but I hurried up the cobbled path to say hello to Father Cosmás before trekking up the cliff in the other direction.

I had only gotten as far as the gate when I saw him walking to meet me. He had chanced to see my arrival from his window high above the boat landing, and had come—as he put it—to welcome me *home*. We visited for a few hours in the guesthouse kitchen, going over, among other things, the new translation of the abbot's book on théosis. I also spoke with him about various goings-on, our mutual friends, and my slow journey to prayer. In familiar form, he listened, said little, and let me express my hopes and my anxieties without criticism. "You know," he said, "once you've begun, you need only continue. Prayer will come." The look on my face must have entertained him. He grinned. Then he smiled broadly, clapping his hands together, adding, "How you feel about it—successful or not successful—really doesn't matter."

I realized that I'd need to set out for Simonópetra, or risk being late for Vespers. Once again, Father Cosmás allowed me to leave behind those belongings I wouldn't need during the next couple days at the monastery above, saving me from hauling them up and back down the steep and rugged trail. With a warm embrace, he wished me well, and handed me an apple "to sweeten" my way.

———

I made pretty good time up the slope, but was fairly winded and, despite the cool weather, dripping wet when, about an hour later, I entered the courtyard beneath the archondaríki. No one was around, but I found a note (printed in Greek and in English) saying that Vespers was underway in the katholikón, inviting me to sit tight or to come on up.

I dug a dry shirt out of my backpack, threw cold water on my face, tried to clean up some, and hurried up the covered causeway to the church.

On Mount Athos, as you must have gathered by now, there is no shortage of beauty; but I have to confess that of all the beauties I have tasted and seen on the Holy Mountain, the beauty of worship at Simonópetra cuts most directly to my heart. This was my first time inside the newly restored katholikón, and so it was my first taste of what I'd call genuine, Simonópetra-style worship.

When my friend Nick Kalaitzandonakes and I had visited earlier in the year, the Vespers service we attended had been in a small chapel deep in Simon's rock—beautiful, to be sure, but fairly dark and subdued. And at that point I hadn't yet experienced enough of the various monasteries to have arrived at anything like a sense of their distinct characters, what might be considered their individual expressions of the common life. This katholikón—bright, airy, marvelously lit, with an array of portable icons fixed to radiant white walls before a brightly polished, golden iconostasis—said a great deal about the character of monastic life at Simonópetra. Some monasteries—I only now began to notice—may emphasize the dark, the severe, and one can't help but feel a certain heaviness in their approach; others take care to emphasize the light, the joyful, and one apprehends an undercurrent of elation in the midst of even their most austere, most grave services.

Both, of course, are beautiful, and meet. Both are powerful. Both are true worship. And as for the fear of God and the love of God, both are palpably present in both sorts of monasteries, but I began, here and now, to suspect a certain . . . what? . . . an emphasis, a prevailing disposition?

Most monasteries, no doubt, lie somewhere in the midst of that spectrum, but Simonópetra is clearly one that foregrounds the love of God, cherishes the joy of religious community, emphasizes the light as they worship the Light.

As Vespers continued, the chanting—probably the most beautiful, certainly the most exuberant on the Holy Mountain—filled that lighted vault with soaring melodies and deep and shifting *isons*—those long-held, low notes that add a heart-stirring vibration throughout the chant. From my stall in the rear of the nave, I glanced over to the choir on the right-hand side, and found the familiar face of Father Iákovos smiling in my direction.

At the dismissal, he came directly over to embrace me. Like Father Cosmás at Grigoríou, Father Iákovos began by welcoming me *home*. He asked about my family as we walked to trápeza together, and we parted at the trápeza entryway—Father Iákovos joining the monks at their tables, and I being led to a table in the middle of the room with a half dozen men who appeared to be monks and visiting clergy. This was the first time I'd ever been seated anywhere but among the other pilgrims, and I wasn't quite sure what to make of it. I supposed that Father Iákovos had arranged this, seeking to make me feel welcomed, and *at home*. That is exactly what I felt.

During the meal, I enjoyed my homecoming, and studied the iconography along the opposite wall. I pretty much inhaled my roasted potatoes, olives, and feta.

From trápeza, we returned to the katholikón to venerate the relics. Once again, I venerated each, and once again, was fully aware that the hand of Mary Magdalene—warm, fragrant, soft—was very like a living hand. Despite its famous dearth of women, I'd have to say that the Holy Mountain occasions a very powerful sense of their presence; the Theotokos, Saint Anna (her mother), and Saint Mary Magdalene (equal to the apostles, as we say) all seem very much *here*, and very much *with us* whenever their names are invoked in prayer, wherever their relics are venerated. I handed the priest a thick wad of prayer ropes—my own and several others I'd picked up in Dáfni for friends back home—so that he might bless them with the relics. When the few pilgrims—maybe seven of us total—had venerated the saints, we were led back to our rooms in the guesthouse.

From there, I hurried back to the archondaríki for a visit with Father Iákovos and Níkos, a novice from America. They were waiting for me at the entryway, and led me back to the guest library, where we settled in for tea, a few sweets, and unhurried conversation.

The evening visit was illuminating in a number of other ways as well. For one, I learned how Simonópetra—suffering from attrition and neglect—had been reestablished in 1973, when the abbot of Great Meteora on mainland Greece arrived with his brotherhood to assist the relative handful of aging and ailing monks who remained here.

This beloved abbot, Yéronda Aimilianós, led his brotherhood to Simonópetra, in part, to escape what had become a bustling tourist destination; they came to the Holy Mountain, that is, to recover their lives of prayer. In the interim, Simonópetra has flourished, remaining relatively small, but developing an astonishing core of highly accomplished monks. As newcomers arrived, Yéronda Aimilianós insisted, as he always had, that his brothers (*and* the sisters of the several convents he has founded and served on the mainland) complete their educations before coming to the monastery to stay. The direct result of that foresight has been a family of scholars, engineers, agriculturalists, and so on who have brought virtually unprecedented levels of professional expertise to the Holy Mountain.

Indirectly, the open-hearted, open-armed, international character of the monastery—and, I'm guessing, the deep, bass note of joy and love that resounds throughout this tower of rock—are other results of the yéronda's insisting upon an educated brotherhood.

The evening's conversation, was, as I say, enlightening.

We turned to other matters. Regarding life on Mount Athos, Níkos said that one of the fathers had told him when he arrived, "We can't promise you a place with no problems; we can only promise you a place without sin."

Father Iákovos nodded, and added, "If we find sin here, it's because we have brought it with us."

As it was getting late by Athonite standards, nearly 10:00 PM, and because I knew the fathers would be rising for their prayers sometime around 2:00 AM, I excused myself, taking with me a book from the visitors bookshelf, *Elder Joseph the Hesychast.*

When I left them, the two were still talking about life on Athos, and I wondered if they would ever get any rest that night.

With the tálanton at 2:30 AM, I found myself being drawn again into the rhythm of the Holy Mountain. Midnight hours, orthros, the Divine Liturgy culminating in the Holy Mysteries—all of them cohering now as one continuous prayer. The immediacy of that sensation gave me to imagine that this really was something of a homecoming. This first liturgy made me wish I could lift the whole katholikón, and set it in Columbia, Missouri. Throughout the worship, I kept thinking of my family back home, aching with the desire that they could be here with me. When time came to partake of the Holy Mysteries, I had a very strong sense that they *were* with me.

Unlike what I'd experienced at other monasteries in the fall, trápeza did not immediately follow the morning liturgy. Instead, Níkos caught me as I left the katholikón, and led me out onto the narrow wooden balcony—one of the several hugging the sheer face of Simonópetra's ancient structure. We leaned on the railing over a drop of about seven hundred feet, peering through the morning dark to the faint lines of whitecaps in the sea, visiting in the darkness as the first glimmer of daylight silhouetted the eastern ridge to the left of our perch.

Níkos said the fathers would be resting for a couple hours before the morning meal, but that coffee would be waiting for us in the archóndariki if I wanted some. I did want some, so we made our way there, finding a few other visitors already enjoying their morning jolts—both coffee and rakí. The loukoúmi remained untouched.

As casually as I could, I asked Níkos about his plans.

Smiling, he told me he might be staying at Simonópetra; he said he had a few things to clear up back home, but expected to return after the holidays, maybe for good.

We left it at that, though I was very keen to hear more about his decision. Something about his candor actually made me careful not to press him; it was coupled, even so, with a curious quality of uncertainty, as if he didn't see where this path would lead him, nor even what he should say about it. Our conversation reminded me of how a poem comes into being: one begins to speak, then trusts the words to lead the way.

We enjoyed our coffee in relative silence, and watched the daylight fill the courtyard.

———

After trápeza, Níkos enlisted me to help with dishwashing. It turned out to be pretty wet work. We donned knee-high rubber boots, strapped on thick rubber aprons, and went at the stacks of stainless steel bowls, platters, and cups. I noticed that the water wasn't especially hot (by the time we were on the last load, in fact, it was actually pretty cold).

I asked Níkos if this was going to pose a health problem. He said he'd asked the same question when he'd started washing dishes some weeks earlier. "Father Iosíf told me it wouldn't kill anybody." He smiled, and kept at sloshing out a stack of bowls. Níkos—I was beginning to notice—shared my taste for irony.

It was a Wednesday, a fasting day, so there'd been no oil in the meal—no oil, therefore, on the plates. They seemed to come pretty clean. I guessed the cold-water wash probably *wouldn't* kill anybody, not today anyway.

When we'd finished and hung up our gear, Níkos let me know that Father Iosíf had asked us to come to the music room for a visit. "He's written a poem," Níkos said. "He'd like you to see it." Again, he was smiling.

Thank God, the poem was actually pretty good, lovely even—a short lyric about sunlight on clouds as seen from the Mount Athos peak. As we talked about the poem, and about many other things, Father Iosíf uncovered a tray he'd brought along, revealing three bowls of jellied fruit—our reward for having helped with dishes.

From there, Níkos led me down to the monastery's actual library—a well-protected though well-lighted vault, deep in the cleft of Simon's Rock. That's where I met Fathers Pávlo and Michael. Both are active scholars, working largely in editing and translation, respectively. It was Father Pávlo, however, who determined to give me a tour, and to lead me through a crash course in modern and contemporary Greek poets.

I confessed to Father Pávlo that the only modern Greek poets I knew well were Elytis, Seféris, and the great Alexandrian Greek, Kaváfy. He approved my selection, but suggested that I was missing out on a great deal. Long story made short, after about two hours of an intensive tutorial, I resurfaced with a list that would surely keep me busy for a good ten years. He also gave me the name of a professor in Thessaloníki whom, he said, I must meet. Later that day, on my way to trápeza, he would pull me aside to give me a letter of introduction addressed to that professor.

I spent most of the remaining afternoon alone. Strolling with the borrowed book in hand, thumbing through it, I slowly realized that this was the same Elder Joseph whose brotherhood had led a restoration of a great many monasteries and sketes here on the Holy Mountain—the same elder, that is, whose young disciple, Yéronda Ephrém, had served as abbot of Philothéou, and now lived in Florence, Arizona, having established some nineteen men's and women's monasteries in the United States.

Among the several photos in the book was one of Elder Joseph's crypt set in a tiny chapel at New Skete, near to Saint Anna's Skete. I determined to visit it during this winter pilgrimage.

That evening, following Vespers, trápeza, and the veneration of the holy relics, Father Iákovos called me to his side and suggested that I meet him later for a visit. I was eager to agree, and he told me how to find his dental office. Besides a range of other duties, Father Iákovos, it turns out, also serves the monastery as its tailor and its dentist. I'm not kidding.

I gave Father Iákovos time to change out of his "church clothes," and into the simpler, working garb, then wandered down the cobbled path to his office. He was waiting for me, seated on the balcony overlooking the sea. He had made tea for us; it was what the monks called mountain tea, which struck me as a mixture of mint, floral herbs, and a stalky item tasting of chamomile.

I figured it was time to cut to the chase. I told Father Iákovos why I'd come. After years of saying the prayer, I still hungered for unceasing prayer; I didn't think I had made much progress—except, perhaps, an increasing hunger to know *always* that sweet sense of God's presence, which I have tasted only fleetingly, intermittently.

To my frank admission, Father Iákovos seemed, initially, startled. Then he smiled. And then he seemed to relax—which probably seems like a funny thing to say about a man whose abiding, genuine calm I had already noted, had already been deeply impressed by. Still, he seemed even more calm now, as he settled back in his chair with a pleasing sense of gravity and with . . . well. . . stillness.

He said, "This is very good." His eyes were shining, his face bright with what I took to be joy. "I'll tell you what I can tell you," he said.

He placed a hand on his chest, just above his abdomen. "You have to hold on to Him," he said, "with all your strength."

He brought his other hand there, too, and then made a tight, cupping gesture with both hands—one above the other—saying, "You have to plead with Him to meet you here," his hands parting now, and opening so that he was making an oval with his forearms—the right arm low across his lower abdomen, the left arm reaching across his chest. He leaned forward and held his arms there, indicating effort, and said, "And when He arrives, you must hold on to him, and not let go."

"Like Jacob," he said, "you must hold on to him."

And then he sat up straight, still holding his arms before him as if to indicate a womb. "And like Jacob," he met my eyes with new intensity, "you will be wounded. Like Jacob, you must say, 'I will not let You go unless You bless me,' and then the wound, the tender hip thereafter, the blessing."

I couldn't talk. I only nodded.

"He is everything," Father Iákovos continued, "and ever-present. He is never *not* here," he said, touching his upper abdomen. "But when you plead to know He's here, and when He answers you, and helps you to meet Him here, you will be wounded by that meeting. The wound will help you know, and that is the blessing."

"I came here to find a spiritual father," I said. "A father to guide me in prayer."

I think he may have blushed.

I saw, at any rate, that I had made him suddenly uncomfortable. "Do you mind," I kept talking, hoping to get through this awkward moment, "if, off and on, I were to write to you, asking questions as they come up?"

He was embarrassed for me, I think. He was searching for words. I had had no idea my clumsy admission would so quickly dissolve the moment of our conversation. "Yes," he said, "you may write." And then, "I say that because I know you won't write unless you must."

I was at a loss. My turn to be embarrassed. "Yes, Father, yes of course. Only if I must."

"You should find a father closer to home," he said.

————

So there it was. Hard on the heels of what was, surely and by far, the most helpful, most illuminating moment of guidance I had yet received on the Holy Mountain—and the first downright mystical experience of my pilgrimage to date—I managed also to bring about one of my journey's most awkward moments. I didn't have a clue, at the time, why Father Iákovos would have so suddenly shut down our conversation the way he seemed to.

I didn't know then, for instance, that Father Iákovos—a monk for many years—was not yet a priest, much less designated a *pnevmatikós*, a confessor. I didn't realize that, perhaps, for those reasons, he was not exactly in a position—by Athonite standards— to offer guidance as a spiritual father.

So, puzzled, feeling suddenly sheepish, and mentally kicking myself for having brought so abruptly to a close this heart-opening conversation with a wonderful and doubtlessly Spirit-bearing monk, I slugged down the rest of my tea, received his warm embrace, and scuttled up the slope to the guesthouse, where I said my prayers and fell into bed.

I kept thinking, *I'm just not ready, not worthy. I* am *kidding myself.*

I bore into the prayer with all the effort I could muster, trying to fend off the approaching, all too familiar melancholy by breathing the Name.

————

My wake-up call rang out on cue, the tálanton resounding through the guesthouse hall this particular morning with unusual energy, like a woodpecker on steroids and speed.

I dressed and hurried out, finding the prayer on my lips. In the dark, I climbed the stone causeway to the katholikón, and settled into my habitual corner before most of the others arrived. One of the younger monks was preparing the lamps and candles, clipping wicks, and readying the hymnals for the readers and chanters.

From behind me, in the exonarthex, I heard the reader begin the prayers. It was at this moment that I felt—as I spoke the words of the Jesus Prayer under my breath—an odd sensation that I had felt only once before.

———

Years before, early on in this business—maybe six months into my adopting the practice of the Jesus Prayer—something happened in my chest. It was my day to stay home and write, and I was home alone. Marcia was out shopping, and Liz and Ben were in school. I had put my books aside, and had been standing before our icon wall, saying the prayer for maybe half an hour, when something strange began—I felt an immediate and pronounced bubbling, a strong fluttering near my heart.

I thought, actually, that I was in serious trouble, that maybe this is what a heart attack might feel like. I stood very still, brought my hands to my heart, and waited for the lights to go out.

The lights didn't go out. The bubbling sensation continued for a few minutes longer, then faded away, leaving me standing there, perplexed but grinning.

I'm not sure how to describe it any better than that, having never even tried to speak of it before, not to anyone. All I can say is that, following this experience, my deliberate repetitions of the prayer have become easier, and that, since then, I've never gone a day without startling to find the prayer circling my thought. From that day, as well, I began to wake at night to find the prayer on my lips.

Even so, as for other desired fruits—an abiding stillness, dispassion, the continuing sense of God's nearness, a conscious charity toward others—these have continued to wax and to wane, to come and to go. When they come, they are very sweet. When they go, it is as though I'm back to square one.

The French monk of the Eastern Church, Father Lev Gillet—among many others who appear to know about these things—cautions us not to depend on feelings to confirm the efficacy of our prayer. Such feelings can be deluding, misleading, even manufactured. In fact, though a sense of the sweetness of prayer—mid-prayer—is a very welcome sense, Father Lev suggests that greater spiritual progress is realized during those dry spells when one perseveres, saying the prayer regardless. "This apparently barren prayer," he writes, "may be more pleasing to God than our moments of rapture, because it is pure from any selfish quest for spiritual delight." It is, he counsels, "a prayer of the plain and naked will."

_____

That moment, at the beginning of services in the katholikón atop Simon's rock, my "prayer of the plain and naked will" seemed to recall that puzzling sensation I'd experienced many years before. This time, I didn't fear a heart attack, but did feel briefly like a spectator of my own experience, noting a trembling, a flutter low in my chest.

Once again, the sensation grew faint, and I wondered if I had only imagined it, though it did leave behind an uncommon awareness of my heart—or of that warm and warming locus just beneath it. That awareness attended me throughout the midnight services, orthros, and became acute at the culmination of Divine Liturgy, when the priest set the body of Christ to my tongue.

_____

After liturgy, I slipped by to my room to rest until trápeza. The book about Elder Joseph lay on the table by my bed, and I pored over it, finding this witness of the elder's teachings recalled by one of his disciples:

_____

As the Holy Fathers tell us in their writings (he always meant Abba Isaak [of Syria] whom he had as his inseparable companion) . . . do not be timid especially now in the beginning when you are starting out, so that you may call forth divine grace. . . . When at last the mind is assured of the presence of help for those who believe, then it enters upon another kind of faith, not the introductory faith as in every believer, but the "faith of contemplation," as the Fathers call it. This is the first stage. . . . Happy will he be if he has someone to guide him and support him and assure him that, by the grace of God, he is making progress.

———

Elder Joseph, by his own admission, had no such helper, but carried with him a volume of Saint Isaak's homilies, from which he received the support and assurance he needed.

———

I was roused from my reading by the bílo ringing us to trápeza. I was the last to arrive, but led again to a place at the center table, where Father George and a few other monks—visitors?—stood awaiting the abbot's prayer.

When the prayer had been said, and the reader began to read from the lives of the saints, we pulled out the benches, and settled in to our breakfast of bean soup. I kept thinking over the counsel of Elder Joseph, his implicit admonition to seek a spiritual guide and his admission that such guidance may be supplied from the Fathers themselves, through their writings.

At the head of our table, Father George, a monk in his eighties, with snow-white hair and beard, ate slowly, thoughtfully. His pleasant face, fixed in a kind smile, seemed almost to glow in the strange morning light of the refectory. At the next table, near the head, Father Iákovos bore a similar demeanor as he picked at his plate. At the other end, the novice Níkos sat with his chin resting on his clasped hands; I was fascinated by his bemused look, wondering what he must be thinking as he surveyed the hall where, if all went according to plan, he would be receiving most of his meals for the rest of his life.

When we'd finished, and the bell was rung, we all filed out between the abbot and his assistants, receiving Yéronda Elisáos's blessing. I hurried from there to my room to gather my things and pack up for the hike down the slope to Grigoríou.

The sky—which had been absolutely clear, teeming with stars, even, when I'd clomped along the wooden balcony on my way to church—had clouded up a good bit during trápeza. By the time I had my gear packed and loaded, the wind had picked up as well, and a sheet of black cloud stretched out across a suddenly gray and choppy Aegean.

I was cinching up the belly strap of my backpack when Father Iákovos found me in the guesthouse; he tapped lightly on the doorframe. He presented me with an English translation of *The Authentic Seal*, the first volume of the collected writings of his former abbot, Yéronda Aimilianós. "Read the second part first; read it right away," he said, "the part on prayer."

And then he handed me a fax from Vatopédi, acknowledging my reservation for a stay there during the following week. "Take this with you, just in case. They sometimes want to see the actual letter."

He walked me down the slope to the edge of the monastery gardens, where we embraced, kissed, and said our farewells. I turned down the footpath, squeezing through a passel of grazing mules. Over the sound of their bells, Father Iákovos called out, "Good journey, Isaák."

The clouds continued to threaten, but the rain didn't arrive until nearly an hour later, as I was entering the gate of Grigoríou for yet another homecoming.

10

the midst of the feast . . .

Father Cosmás was washing cups in the archondaríki kitchen when I arrived, dropping my pack to the stone floor of the balcony. "Isaák!" he hollered, and raising a finger to say *just a minute*, immediately set to brewing a pot of drip coffee for us to share. As he scooped out enough ground coffee for a good stiff pot, he commenced asking about my time up the slope.

Winter on Athos brings its own array of pleasures, especially for me. The rains, the low clouds, and wafting mists all bring to mind the landscape of my youth, the landscape of my imagination—that strip of evergreen forest between the Cascade Range and the Puget Sound of Washington State. And the ready offer of hot coffee—and lots of it—was perfectly in keeping with that scene.

I told Father Cosmás about meeting Níkos, and about my amazing visit with Father Iákovos. He, too, loved the way Father Iákovos had invoked Jacob in describing the way we must—as he now put it—"insist" on knowing God's presence.

Over our cups, I pulled out my map and asked Father Cosmás to help me plan the rest of my trip. I knew that after my two nights at Grigoríou I'd be heading to Saint Anna's Skete, but after that things were still pretty much up in the air.

His first thoughts were, "The Feast of Saint Andrew! You must go to Saint Andrew's Skete for the vigil Sunday night!"

Done.

Like Father Iákovos, he also suggested that I try to get to Vatopédi; I showed him the fax that Father Iákovos had given me, to which he responded, "Perfect."

So, with the map spread out on the kitchen table, we charted a course that would take me from Grigoríou to Saint Anna's Skete, where

I would spend Saturday night and celebrate Sunday liturgy. From there, I would hike the coastal trail to New Skete (where I would stop to pray at Elder Joseph's tomb), proceeding on to Saint Paul's Monastery, where I would catch the boat to Dáfni, and take the bus to Karyés. I would arrive in time to settle in to Saint Andrew's Skete for my first Athonite vigil on Sunday night. Father Cosmás urged me to try to return to Grigoríou as well, pointing out that my last night on the Holy Mountain would, coincidentally, be the night of their vigil for the Feast of Saint Nicholas.

The rest of that afternoon and the following day afforded a chance to be especially deliberate about prayer, and deliberate about cultivating the stillness that had become intermittently available to me. I began to notice, during this time, something else about prayer and stillness in my life. Neither had developed in ways that were noticeable from day to day, but I could not deny that they *were* developing. The *way*—it now became clearer to me—was inevitably a slow one, with prayer and stillness becoming only slightly more apprehensible as you go.

Saint Anna's Skete

After trápeza on Saturday morning, I packed up, again leaving spare clothing and books with Father Cosmás. I boarded the *Ágia Ánna* for Saint Anna's Skete, and studied the shoreline as I went, passing Dionysíou, Saint Paul's, and New Skete along the way. From the arsanás of Saint Anna's, the hike to the skete was more demanding—more unremittingly steep—than even the rugged trail rising from Grigoríou to Simonópetra. In less than a quarter mile "as the crow flies," the gain in elevation was easily over a thousand feet.

It took me more than an hour to reach the gate—stopping to gasp at nearly every switchback, and, off and on, stepping aside for recurring strings of pack mules hauling goods from the boat. Passing beneath the icon of Saint Anna and the Theotokos over the gate, I crossed myself, bowed low to the icon, and stumbled in.

There was only one person in the courtyard, a monk filling oil lamps near the pergola. He looked up and said matter-of-factly, "Hey, I recognize that face."

It was Father Seraphim himself.

"Evlogeíte," I said, approaching to kiss his hand. "I'm Isaák."

"Yes," he said, "you are." He looked up from the oil lamp in his hand. "I got your letter."

From home between journeys—about two months earlier—I had written him about my search for a spiritual father, my desire for prayer. "Yes," I said, "I hoped you had." I didn't say it just then, but I had also hoped he would have written back in the meantime.

Finishing with the lamps, and mopping up the good bit of oil he'd spilled on the stone wall, he said, "Come, I'm ready for coffee; I'll bet you are, too."

As we sat in the kitchen, I learned that he was preparing to make a trip himself, heading to New York to meet with some elder or other regarding his work, a history of Orthodoxy in America. "Travel makes me uneasy," he said. "I'm afraid I'm a little preoccupied with this trip, too distracted to be of much help to you."

Another puzzlement. Another minor disappointment.

We chatted a bit longer, mostly making small talk about mutual friends back in the States.

"I think your room is ready for you. I'll take you to it."

I followed him to the same room I had shared with Sohsen three months earlier.

"Have a rest," he said. "Perhaps we can visit later on."

As it turned out, we never did.

Father Theóphilos showed up later in the day just as a group of pilgrims—six Greek men carrying suitcases—arrived from New Skete. He led us to the katholikón, where we venerated the relics—the spice-scented foot of Saint Anna among them—and where I venerated the miracle-working icon of the saint. The icon was surrounded by a fresh batch of miracles—children's photos, thank-you gestures from dozens of new parents.

I went directly to my room after trápeza, and stood for a while on the balcony outside my window. Evening was settling in, and a covey of doves was circling the skete as if lost. When I could no longer follow their circling in the deepening dusk, I returned to my bed, puzzling over my search, feeling once again a little discouraged, but falling asleep with the prayer on my lips.

I woke well before the midnight service, and, because the weather had taken a cold turn, I bundled up before heading to the courtyard. From the terrace there, I watched the clouds race across the sky over the sea, alternately revealing and obscuring the brilliant field of stars behind them. When I heard chanting wafting up on the wind from somewhere down the dark slope below, I made my way to the cemetery chapel.

Inside, a solitary priest was preparing the altar; he was saying his prayers aloud, and didn't notice my slipping in. I found my familiar stall in the left corner of the nave, and settled into prayers of my own.

In time, Father Theóphilos showed up to assist the priest, and a chanter arrived minutes later. By the time we were ready to begin the midnight prayers, one more monk had arrived, as had one other pilgrim—six men total.

It was a very sweet service, slow-moving and quiet, a series of prayers spanning most of four hours, but seamlessly arriving at the Holy Mysteries, which I received in this tiny chapel, actually trembling.

———

Outside again, now in grey daylight, I inhaled the crisp air deeply, waking to a curious sensation of hope. Father Seraphim was nowhere to be found, Father Theóphilos and the other monks had dispersed to their kéllia, and I had a long day—including a good hike—ahead of me, but I felt, frankly, cheerful. There wasn't any breakfast to be had, so I filled my water bottle and hit the trail. It was, all else aside, Sunday morning—a likely enough day for resurrecting hope.

In less than an hour, I came to the fork leading down the slope to New Skete and made my descent, following a grip of half a dozen mules who insisted on staying a few steps ahead of me, even as they continued to browse on the salal.

——— *New Skete* ———

Twenty minutes later, the trail led onto a dirt road, where I found a workman notching rails for a fence. "*Pou ine to táfos yia Yéronda Iosíf?*" I asked in crappy Greek, seeking directions to Elder Joseph's tomb. He rattled off a sentence or two I didn't understand, but pointed as he did so. I set out in the direction he was pointing.

In minutes, I was standing outside the tiny chapel where Elder Joseph the Hesychast lay reposed. It was a whitewashed stone hut with a red tile roof—much smaller than I had imagined—T-shaped, with the narthex facing the sea and forming the wide end, and the narrow length comprising the nave, which held the elder's crypt along its left-hand side.

The door actually had a key in it, but turn it however I tried, the lock wouldn't budge. I hoped this wasn't some kind of sign that I had no business here. The windows lining the hut, even so, were open, and, peering through each in turn, I walked around the chapel. Then, I knelt at the front, settling into the prayer.

The stillness there was very sweet. I knelt for a good long while, and, intermittently, as I prayed, I also asked the elder to help me in my search for a spiritual guide.

———

When I had climbed back to the main trail, the wind had picked up again, sending thick bands of black clouds west to east as I hustled along the trail. The rain, when it came, was light and actually refreshing, and helped me to make pretty good time on my way to the Monastery of Saint Paul. Still, I was feeling pretty weak when I entered the monastery canyon, so I didn't walk all the way up to the monastery this time. Instead, I stopped in to venerate the icons at the small shrine midway up, the spot where the gifts of the Magi had been presented to the fathers.

I was pretty hungry by this time—suddenly a little dizzy, even—but all I had on hand was water, and not really much of that. On the other hand, the *Ágia Ánna* would be pulling into the pier soon, and I could grab a bite on board. I rested at the shrine as long as I could, then, continuing the prayer, found the wide gravel road to the arsanás, and made it down in time for the boat.

Once on board, I bought two bottles of water, a hot "*Nescafe me gala*," and a "toast," a popular snack made by stuffing a fat, soft hoagie roll with kasseri cheese and ham, then smashing it flat between two searing iron griddles until it crisps. After a few bites of the delicacy, my dizziness went away.

Again, it hit me how few men, relatively speaking, were on the boat—maybe a dozen, not counting the crew. A few months earlier, the *Ágia Ánna* carried well over a hundred each time I was aboard. The wind had picked up again, the whitecaps rising across the sea, the spray blowing up clear to the upper deck. As we plowed along—with rough and rolling stops at Dionysíou, Grigoríou, and Simonópetra—I could tell by the looks on the faces of the crew that, due to the weather, this could well be the last run for a while.

———

Dáfni was nearly deserted. Most of the shops were open, but for the most part there weren't any pilgrims inside. The bus to Karyés (and to Saint Andrew's Skete, where I'd been directed by Father Cosmás) wouldn't be leaving until the ferry from Ouranoúpolis arrived, so I grabbed another coffee at the café, found a likely table on the patio, and settled in to read for a while from Yéronda Aimilianós's *The Authentic Seal*.

Half an hour later, however, with the arrival of the *Áxion Estín*, the scene was suddenly changed. Evidently, the feast day of Saint Andrew (whose Old Calendar date correlates to our December 12) had filled the boat to capacity, and easily three hundred men poured over the gangway to the pier—many of them priests and monks from mainland Greece and elsewhere. They made a beeline for the buses—shoving and shouting just like the good old days last summer—so, grabbing my pack I joined the stampede, not wanting to be left behind.

———

Saint Andrew's Skete, as I mentioned, is immense, comparable to some of the larger monastery enclaves. Most of it is also uninhabitable. Of the dozen or more four- and five-story buildings that constitute its expanse across a broad Athonite hilltop, maybe three of them—as well as the enormous kyriakón, the largest church on Mount Athos—are in use, and the renovations of those few are not entirely finished. Most often, the skete will accommodate twenty to thirty pilgrims at a time; on the feast day of a monastery or skete, however, tradition has it that no one is turned away. The logistical dilemma then—for the two dozen monks who live there—was *where* to put their five hundred guests. A surprising number of these guests, it seemed to me, turned out to be Russian.

When I arrived, the hallways were already lined with cots and blankets, as were the walls of the guesthouse chapel, and those of the guesthouse dining hall. And already, at three in the afternoon, most of those cots had men or boys sleeping in them, resting for the all-night vigil that would commence at around 8:00 PM.

In other words, the place was packed with monks, priests, and pilgrims either sitting, standing, or stretched out snoring. The few monks assigned to finding rooms for us all seemed almost giddy at how impossible their job had suddenly become; their good humor did a lot to keep the whole fiasco pleasant.

And the long wait turned out to be ideal for prayer; in fact, the nearly absurd circumstance actually helped me disengage, settle in, and find stillness in the midst of the bustle.

Long story short: I stood in the entry hall with my backpack from 3:00 PM until 5:00 PM, when we were all called to trápeza. Thereafter, I found my place again and stood waiting until 9:00 PM, when a Russian monk—actually a novice from St. Petersburg—who had been given a room some hours earlier saw that I was still there and cornered the guestmaster. From where I stood, I could see the man gesturing at me and pointing away down the hallway he'd just exited.

In another five minutes, I was following the two of them to the room I would share with Viktor, the Russian novice, and, for starters, one other man. Along the way, we walked by lantern light through what looked like bombed-out ruins, crossing planks and ascending fractured staircases to a wing that still had most of its roof. Of the rooms in our wing, our room was the only one with glass in most of the window panes; the missing pane had been replaced with a square of wool blanket. The temperature inside the room was well below 40 degrees; fortunately, each bed held a stack of three heavy blankets.

The other man was also a monk; Hieromonk Prochor had been Viktor's childhood friend, and was now a priest-monk. From what I gathered, both served the Valaam monastery—the "Mount Athos of the north"—at its pilgrim offices in St. Petersburg.

Father Prochor didn't speak much English, but Viktor was nearly fluent. We were able to visit briefly as I hurried to stow my things and join them on their way to the vigil, which was already well underway. As we prepared to leave, the door was opened and there stood the guestmaster with yet another monk. My two roommates went to him immediately and kissed his hand. I gathered that he was a hierarch from Valaam itself.

Because Victor's Greek was negligible and because the guestmaster knew little Russian, they conversed in fairly followable English, and I was, therefore, able to witness a curious scene.

The hierarch—though a relatively young-looking man—looked a bit puzzled by the state of the room to which he'd been led. The guestmaster asked Viktor, "Is the room OK with Vladika?" Viktor asked the hierarch, who seemed to be struggling to say yes. He nodded, he looked around, he half-smiled, he shrugged, then said, according to Victor, "Yes, it's OK."

The guestmaster rocked on his heels a bit, clearly embarrassed. He said to Viktor, "Please tell Vladika that it's all we have." Viktor told him, and the vladika softened immediately, trying hard to appear more sincere as he assured us all that the room was just fine.

We left the vladika with the lantern to prepare for the vigil—during which, it turned out, he was to be part of a number of hierarchical processions—and followed the guestmaster through the maze that would lead to the courtyard, and from there to the kyriakón.

———

I had been around the outside of this kyriakón a couple times already in the past, first when Nick Kalaitzandonakes and I had wandered the skete during my first journey in September, and then as I'd first arrived here earlier in the day. I'd even been *under* it; the expansive, main trápeza is located in the basement beneath the nave. Walking around it and eating beneath it had given me a hint as to how huge the church would be, but nothing prepared me for the sparkling reality within.

The kyriakón itself is, without question, the largest on the Holy Mountain, it's gold-layered iconostasis reaching more than 180 feet across, easily fifty feet high, and the nave itself stretching well over a hundred yards. The intricacy and beauty of the wood carvings and iconography are mind-boggling. Its dozens of pillars each bear four or more larger-than-life-sized icons—the Theotokos, Christ, countless saints. Clearly, the kyriakón itself is what the monks of Saint Andrew's Skete have been pouring their hearts into restoring over the past several years.

On this night, the golden candelabrum before the altar—easily twenty-five feet in diameter and stretching more than thirty feet from top to bottom—was aflame with more than a hundred thick, beeswax tapers (perhaps a hundred more were not yet lit). Another candelabrum, nearly as big, stood, for the moment unlit, midway in the nave, standing above the Gospel stand; each choir—that is, the twin arms of the cross, to the left and right of the central candelabrum—held another just slightly smaller than the Gospel fixture; these, too, were not yet lit.

As the chanting continued from the right choir, I lit my own three candles in the narthex, and began venerating icons. I did so for more than half an hour, finally reaching the thirty or so that spread across the width before the iconostasis. Among these icons, midway along those to the right of the Royal Doors, the skull of Saint Andrew lay—the color of beeswax—in a golden chest. I touched the floor before it, and kissed its fragrant brow. I removed my prayer rope from my wrist, and touched it to the holy relic.

Leaving the icons, I found a likely stall (there are more than a thousand of these *stasídthi* here) near the front of the nave, and settled in to pray.

———

The night was, for the most part, very like a dream. A dream of prayer. That continuous prayer was . . . *troubled?* . . . *softened?* . . . maybe *slowed*, occasionally by a fresh beauty that brought me—each time it happened—*almost* to the surface of consciousness. This is very hard to write about. I was not *unconscious*, but I found my attention fixed, for the most part, to the prayer, and slightly less fixed to the hymns and actions of the monks. Candles were lit while others were snuffed and eventually relit in a profoundly Byzantine sequence that I observed as if it had happened long ago. Processions came and went. And all night long I said the prayer. It seemed as if I couldn't *not* say it.

At certain points, I seemed to see it.

During several festal hymns, the huge candelabra were fully lit and—with great labor from monks pushing with long steel poles—set into motion, circling in broad, expanding circles. As they spun—like wheels within wheels—the gold-layered iconostasis and the hundreds of golden stands and fixtures throughout the abysmally enormous nave caught that golden light and flickered as if themselves aflame. The air seemed filled with light.

When finally—near 4:00 AM I'm guessing—the service grew still, and most of the candles were extinguished, I surfaced.

I looked around and saw that the hundreds of worshipers had dwindled to a handful. I saw that the handful were, for the most part, very old monks, dozing in their stalls.

I venerated the icons before the iconostasis, and the skull of Saint Andrew (though the golden chest was now closed), and walked out into the very cold night.

———

The sky was exceedingly clear, filled with stars, and sporting what looked to be a frost ring circling the moon. I was shivering powerfully when I finally found my way to the room. I took off only my boots, and crawled beneath the heavy blankets. I must have fallen asleep immediately.

A few hours later, I was awakened by Viktor coming in to tell me that the Divine Liturgy was starting soon, and that he knew I'd want to be there. I followed his penlight through the dark of our ruined wing, and down the creaking staircase. Outside, the sky was just beginning to pale in the east.

The kyriakón was almost fully lit again, and it appeared that everyone had returned. The hierarchical liturgy—including more than twenty priests in procession—was extravagantly beautiful, and as we lined up for the Eucharist, it seemed to me that we were well over five hundred strong.

I received the Holy Mysteries, and turned to find both an enormous platter of antídoron and another even larger platter of heavy bread soaked in what must have been sweet wine.

From there, our crew of five hundred lined up to receive the bishop's blessing, lined up to venerate the icons, and exited to the courtyard where we lined up for trápeza. Even if I hadn't already noted that many of these visitors were Russian, the fact of their lining up for *anything* should have told me they probably weren't Greek.

Eventually, we were all fed. Though it was a Monday (usually a fasting day for the monks), the Feast of Saint Andrew trumped the fast, and we enjoy potatoes with fish, feta, and olives—not to mention one of my favorite Athonite innovations: wine with breakfast. After trápeza, we were each given a small icon (mine was of Saint Athanásios, founder of *Megístis Lávras*), and a sack of cookies, and sent on our way. Most waited for the several buses that would take them back to Dáfni and the boat. I hiked the half mile to Karyés, and hurried to the Pilgrim Office, arriving just as it opened. There, I was able to add another six days to my diamonitírion. The officer was not the same I'd seen on my last journey, but was eager to ask pretty much the same questions as his colleague had in September: *Are you Greek? Is your mother Greek?* This time my answers brought a handshake and a grin instead of a shrug.

I turned from there to the café and bought a coffee (*black* coffee—no milk—because the Feast of Saint Andrew evidently didn't figure quite so prominently on the café owner's calendar as it did half a mile down the road). Sipping and resting, I studied the map to plan my next move. Father Iákovos had faxed my request for a night at Vatopédi, so pretty much all I knew was that I would need to arrive there on Wednesday. That left me two days and two nights of meantime. I was also very sleepy; the coffee wasn't making much of a dent in the fact that I hadn't slept but a few hours the night before. So, not knowing much about the nearby Koutloumousíou Monastery, I set out to walk the quarter mile or so that would take me to its gate.

————

Koutloumousíou ranks sixth in the hierarchy of the Athos community, and dates back to sometime before 1169. Among its treasures are more than 650 manuscripts (many of them illuminated) and over 3,500 printed books. For this reason, it is a favorite stop for ecclesiastical scholars.

For this reason, perhaps, the monks there seem to be somewhat protective of their enclave—as least insofar as pilgrims without reservations go.

When, crossing myself, I entered the gate, I found the door to a very plush, very comfortable archondaríki immediately to my left. I entered, dropped my pack with a thud, and waited for the guestmaster to arrive. When he hurried in a few minutes later, he let me know there was no room for me. I asked about other nights that week, and he said there was no room anytime soon.

Still, he asked me to sit, and he brought me a tray of water, loukoúmi, and rakí. I took the chance to study the map, and realized that I would need to hike for at least a couple hours to get to Pantokrátoros on the eastern shore, where I may or may not find a place.

As I prepared to go, I saw that the katholikón doors were open, so I asked if I might venerate the icons before I left.

The change on the guestmaster's face was immediate. He lit up, nodded, "*Nai, nai!* You come now."

I followed him into the glassed-in exonarthex, entered the narthex, the nave, and moved from icon to icon, venerating each in turn. Like every Athonite church, it is cruciform, beautiful, slightly smaller than some, but wonderfully *full*, laden with a lush, sweet weight. This is especially true of the small chapel to the left of the narthex, dedicated to the Protection of the Theotokos, and containing a very beautiful—and, I gathered, miracle-working—icon of the Theotokos.

Evidently, something about my response to his katholikón and its icons gave the guestmaster a revised impression of me, perhaps a less jaded appraisal of this particular pilgrim. When we'd returned to the archondaríki, I bent to lift my pack and found his hand pushing it back to the cobbled walkway. "*Ohi*," he said, "you have room here."

"*Símera i ávrio?*" I asked. "Today or tomorrow?"

"*Nai*," he said, "*símera*." And with that he led me across the courtyard and up to the guesthouse on the second floor, opening the door to a lovely, cozy room overlooking the footpath to Philothéou. There didn't seem to be many other guests around; I had the double room to myself.

"I will tell you now the program," he said. "The Vespers is at 4:30, then trápeza. And we wake you at 2:00 in the night."

"*Nai, nai, nai, efharistó*," I said, bowing to kiss his hand.

He stopped me mid-bow, pulling back his hand, and saying of himself, "Just the monk." He closed the door behind him as he left.

Surprised and happy at this turn of events, I relaxed enough to finally feel the toll of the vigil. My legs felt like lead, and my eyes were suddenly heavy. I washed my face, downed an entire half-liter bottle of water, knelt to thank Christ and the Theotokos for a shorter walk than I had feared, and settled in for a nap.

———

The afternoon and evening went pretty much as expected, a lovely Vespers—though there were, at most, a dozen monks and four pilgrims present—a meal of bean soup, stewed kale with vinegar, and bread, and after trápeza a chance to venerate the relics. Afterward, still somewhat numb-skulled from the all-night vigil, I went directly to my room, said my prayers, and was asleep in minutes.

———

As promised, the tálanton rang out shortly after 2:00 AM, calling us to the midnight hours. These blended into orthros and then, as orthros was concluding, I felt a tug on my sleeve. The guestmaster was pulling all the pilgrims out before the Divine Liturgy began. I was pretty confused, and wondered if this would be yet another instance of my-not-being-Greek leading someone to assume I wasn't sufficiently Orthodox.

Wrong.

That wasn't it at all.

We were led across the courtyard, up three creaking flights of stairs, and into a tiny chapel at the top of one of the corner towers. Inside, we celebrated the Divine Liturgy in what was becoming my favorite fashion—an intimate chapel service with one priest and one psalti. Presumably because it was a Monday, none of the monks received Communion, but unlike some fasting-day liturgies I'd witnessed, here at Koutloumousíou, the priest seemed to pause with the Holy Mysteries, seeming actually to invite us to the cup. Most of the pilgrims remained in their stalls, but three of us eagerly received.

Frequent Communion, to be honest, is a relatively recent return to an ancient practice. For most "cradle Orthodox" in most of the world, Communion has become a once- or twice-a-year event. They—and their parents and grandparents before them—were raised to believe that receiving the Holy Mysteries was to be preceded by a week of strict fasting and by the sacrament of confession; to partake of the body of Christ without such preparation was considered to be "partaking unworthily."

More recently, the thinking has emphasized that, for one, no one is ever able to partake in any state *except* unworthily; it is our partaking that assists in our worthiness. So, while fasting before Communion is encouraged (one does not receive any food prior to the morning liturgy), and while confession is expected (generally several times each year, and at least once during Great Lent), the emphasis has fallen upon the words that invite us to the cup: *with faith, love, and the fear of God, draw near.*

With faith, love, and the fear of God, *and* quite unworthily, several of us accepted the invitation to receive the Holy Mysteries of Christ.

———

After trápeza, I thanked the guestmaster for his kindness, and headed back to Karyés to make a phone call on the card phone. I reached the guestmaster at Pantokrátoros and asked about a place for the night. He said, "Yes, but hurry. We fill up."

I told him I'd be walking from Karyés. "Walking?" he asked. "OK, give me your name; we fill up."

It turned out that I was in for another feast day, and another all-night vigil.

This would be a vigil for the Feast of the *Gerontissa*, a miracle-working icon of the Theotokos, which uniquely depicts the Panagía in her old age.

Before any of this would happen, however, I had a good four hours of hiking ahead of me, about three of which would be under a gray sky and in a constant, light rain. Dreary as that may sound, for this Puget Sound native, it was actually a very savory trek.

11

Peace, be still.

The hike took me, for the most part, along winding dirt roads, descending into misted valleys and climbing to high ridges, each of which offered successive, cloud-laden vistas of the Holy Mountain's interior and a startling number of hermitages and modest monastic enclaves.

There are any number of maps of Mount Athos available. I learned on my first pilgrimage that there is only one map worth having, a detailed topographic map drawn by Reinhold Zwerger of Austria. I held this map in my left hand as I walked; I held my prayer rope in my right.

At one comic moment about an hour into my hike, I looked up from my map to see a man approaching from, I learned, Pantokrátoros. He was bearded (like me), dressed in black jeans and a black shirt (as was I), and he also carried his prayer rope in his right hand and Zwerger's map in his left. As we approached each other, it dawned on us what an uncanny, mirror image we composed. We met laughing.

He was Father John, a novice monk—maybe ten years my junior—from Saint John the Baptist Monastery in Essex, England. He'd been sent to Mount Athos by his abbot in order, as he said it, "to finally learn some Greek." He told me about a fork in the road ahead that would save me some time—a narrow dirt road to the left that wasn't on the map—and we parted wishing each other well.

Two hours into my trek, the road wound along the ridge above the northern coastline. I saw, some distance to the south, what I knew to be the monastery of Stavroníkita, and realized that I must have missed the turn for which I had been watching. That's also when the wind and rain picked up with surprising force; the sea before me was a wild gray-green expanse laced with whitecaps. The wind roared up—with alternating gusts of warm and cold—through the slope of pine, cypress, and chestnut. Scanning the seascape, I noted that the familiar fleet of fishing boats and ferries was nowhere to be seen. I wondered—for the first time, actually—if I would have trouble leaving as I'd planned to do, in five day's time.

As I followed the road around a major headland, I caught my first glimpse of Pantokrátoros, poised on another headland far to the north. The rain, I began to notice, now had snow in it.

I was fairly soaked and chilled to the bone as I descended to the monastery grounds. I found a footpath that promised to save me a little time, and wandered over a footbridge near the arsanás, then up several swtichbacked slopes of cobbled mule road, and finally around the ancient wall to find the entryway. Pantokrátoros was noticeably under repair; much of the interior courtyard was skirted by scaffolding, and several lengths of the interior structure were without an inward-facing wall. The katholikón itself was about halfway into its new coat of wine-colored stucco.

I found the archondaríki just across the courtyard from where I'd entered, but the door was locked. In minutes, however, a voice behind me said, "*Iste Isaák?*" It was the guestmaster, newly returned from depositing a group of pilgrims in their rooms. In English, Father Ioánis said, "I have you a bed. This way, please." Then, he said, "Isaák, you all wet!"

He did indeed have me a bed, up two flights in a room facing the sea, which by now had become absolutely wild. My bed actually rested against the broad sill of the seaside window, and as I peered out, I could see the surf churning directly below our room, which hung out a bit over the granite cliff. Sea spray was being blown on a stiff wind directly up that cliff and up three stories of monastery to fleck our windows with foam.

My roommates were three men from Thessaloníki and two from Romania. As we rested, stoking the in-room woodstove and sharing stories and family photos, each of my roommates took care to inform me that while they liked individual Americans quite a bit, they were very angry with America, specifically with our president, George W. Bush. Once I'd made clear that for the most part we held these passions in common, the conversation moved on to other things, and the afternoon passed pleasantly enough.

The call to Vespers came around 3:30 PM, and we all made our way to the katholikón, joined along the way by a good thirty or so pilgrims, nearly fifty monks, and a dozen or more young men in seminary cassocks. These last were visiting from the mainland to serve as the choir for the festal celebration. Only twenty or so monks live at Pantokrátoros year-round, but their numbers were increased for the feast day by representatives from many other monasteries, in particular from Xenofóndos, with whom the monks of Pantokrátoros maintain a strong connection; the abbot of Xenofóndos, Yéronda Aléxios, would be celebrating the festal vigil and liturgy.

The katholikón is relatively small, but exudes—as, frankly, every katholikón on the Holy Mountain exudes—a lush presence, a fullness, even when few worshipers are within. This katholikón has, moreover, a split narthex, the smaller, left-hand side of which serves as entry to a small, powerfully *full* chapel, dedicated to the Dormition of the Theotokos.

It was in the smaller narthex outside this chapel where I was introduced to Father Zakarías. I had already found a stall inside the nave when Father Ioánis, the guestmaster, found me, tugging on my arm to follow him. "American monk, you come," he said.

Father Zakarías stood among several monks who had just arrived from Xenofóndos; he had been assisting his abbot in preparations for the vigil. I could see that he was still quite busy.

"I'm Isaák," I said, "from the States."

He grinned—unsurprised, it seemed to me—and said, "Zakarías. I'm from Florida." Father Zakarías appeared to be in his late twenties or early thirties, tall, kind-faced, his brown beard already showing a little gray. We spoke only briefly, but he asked where I would be stopping over the remainder of my pilgrimage. When I mentioned that I'd planned two nights at Vatopédi and two at Grigoríou, he said, "If you have a night to spare, please come see us at Xenofóndos."

I promised I would.

Back in the nave, the Vespers continued, and I saw that while the young seminarians filled the right-hand choir, the monks of the monastery took their positions in the left. There were a good number of younger monks among the resident choir, so the contrast was not so great; still, one or two of the older monks appeared to be *very* old, and one in particular—who was asked to chant a number of hymns by himself—seemed ancient, like a small and knotty oak. He didn't appear to have many teeth, so he clearly struggled to pronounce the words of the hymns; his voice, even so, was sweet, if a little shaky.

Both choirs sang the other hymns with vigor and passion, and the service went by very quickly. I was surprised at how quickly.

After trápeza, we were able to venerate the relics there, then were chased out so that the preparations could continue for the vigil. I and most of my roommates lay down to rest for the long night ahead.

———

At around 8:30, the tálanton called us to begin again. The two choirs led us through the night with hardly a letdown in their energy; even the subdued cycles of the vigil were passionately chanted. Yéronda Aléxios—whose tenor voice was like an angel's—joined them and accepted the invitation to chant many of the solo hymns. The candelabra were fully fired up, made to swing in their vertiginous arcs and circles, and the vigil was celebrated with astonishing beauty. Late into the night, I experienced again the curious hallucinations that had troubled me—intermittently *frightened* me—during my first pilgrimage. I would close my eyes to find someone standing before me, speaking words I could not quite gather.

This time, I was not frightened, but tried to hear what was being said.

At one such time, I must have fallen asleep in my stall. When I woke again—early in the morning—orthros was well underway.

I felt a little embarrassed at having fallen asleep, but I also felt elated that I had stayed, surrounded by worship, throughout the entire night. Not long after, the liturgy began—a hierarchical liturgy with Abbot Aléxios and eight other priests—with renewed freshness, and was as sweet a worship as I have ever tasted. When it was time for the Creed to be recited, the very old and mostly toothless monk from the left-hand choir stood forward, and, taking great pains to speak as clearly as he could, spoke the Creed, "the Symbol of the Faith," with a confidence and conviction such as I have never heard before or since.

I was not the only one shaken by this. Where he sat in the bishop's throne, Yéronda Aléxios raised a hand to wipe his eyes.

I partook of the Eucharist in a flood of gratitude, and passing from the cup to the table of antídoron, stopped to venerate the icon of the Gerontissa, whose vigil we had kept.

———

From trápeza, I bid farewell to my roommates, saddled up my heavy pack, and set out for Vatopédi up the coast. The rain had stopped, but the wind was brisk, and the long hike itself—along a forested trail and a stretch of muddy dirt road—effected a wonderful recovery from the long night. Sleepy after breakfast, I was wide awake and savoring the damp air, the cold wind, and—gusting, every so often—a warm breath of wet earth with a hint of spring in it.

Just over two hours later, I was descending the crushed rock road of winding switchbacks that would lead to Vatopédi, an expansive fortress poised at the sea-end of a wide valley sloping to the Aegean. From the top of that descent, I gathered that I had the better part of an hour of hiking yet to go. Instead, a Land Rover roared up from behind and pulled to the side of the road ahead of me. It was a Mount Athos policeman—a curious phenomenon, in any event—and he had stopped to offer me a lift.

Officer Yórgos asked me where I'd walked from. When I told him I'd just come from Pantokrátoros, he said, "Dangerous, too dangerous to walk alone." This was the first time anyone had said any such thing to me. "Here?" I asked. "Dangerous? Mount Athos?"

"Anywhere," he said. "Here is no different."

"Since when?" I asked.

"Since the fall from the garden." He was grinning.

I figured he had found the right line of work.

As we pulled up near the entry to Vatopédi, I thanked Yórgos for the ride, and for his advice. He wished me a good journey, and strongly suggested I use the microbus for the ride back.

—— *The Monastery of Vatopédi* ——

Vatopédi is, I'm guessing, the most well protected on the Holy Mountain. If you arrive—as most pilgrims do—by way of the main road from Karyés, you'll pass a guarded checkpoint more than a mile from the monastery gate; unless your name is on their list of pilgrims with reservations, you won't get any closer than that. The monastery gate itself is perhaps the most carefully controlled on Mount Athos; for instance, this is the only monastery where I actually had to hand over my diamonitírion, which the gatekeeper then called to verify. For a number of reasons—not the least of which is the fact that Britain's Prince Charles is a frequent visitor here—Vatopédi is a very busy monastery, bustling with many monks, visiting clergy, and pilgrims. The guest area sports a machine—actually *two* of them—that will automatically brew Greek coffee to the pilgrim's customized taste: *glykó, métrio, skéto*—sweet, middling, or pure. Moreover, like Simonópetra, Vatopédi manifests a decidedly international flavor (a good number of Cypriots), and is profoundly—once you've cleared both gates—very welcoming to guests who have reservations.

One other item of what I considered to be of increasing interest: Abbot Ephrém, the abbot of Vatopédi—like Yéronda Ephrém of Philothéou and of Saint Anthony's Monastery in Arizona—is the spiritual child of Elder Joseph the Hesychast, about whom I'd been reading during my stay at Simonópetra.

Once inside, I found my way to the waiting room where a roaring woodstove was keeping off the chill from the sea. The guestmaster found my name on the list, and asked if I would like a place on the microbus to Karyés the next day. He then asked—much to my surprise—if I wished to see a priest for confession.

"You have a priest who speaks English?" I asked.

"Yes, *kyrie*, of course."

I wasn't ready for this. Confession remains, as I've said, a scary proposition. Still, without thinking much about it, I said yes.

"Very good," the monk said. "I will find you during Vespers, and take you to Father Gregory."

He led me to my room, an amazing little studio apartment, complete with kitchenette; I saw that I would be staying here alone. The guesthouse at Vatopédi is more like a European hotel than any of the guest quarters I had yet been in, with common washrooms at either end of the hall, but with absolutely pristine two- and four-person rooms, all of them apparently remodeled quite recently.

My purpose in coming to Vatopédi was to pray. During my last conversation with Father Iákovos, he had encouraged me to come here; and, as I mentioned, he had faxed my request to the guestmaster himself. For all I knew, his personal arrangements had led to this solitary room, where I might spend uninterrupted hours in prayer. Now that I knew I would also be making confession in the evening, I was all the more eager to settle in and prepare for that opportunity.

————

Late in the afternoon, the tálanton stirred me from my meditation, and called us all to Vespers. Inside the katholikón—clearly one of the most richly ornate on the Holy Mountain—I found that the monks had set up actual chairs for the pilgrims to use. The central nave is wide enough that they were able to place three rows of wooden chairs on either side of the passage between the choirs and the narthex while still leaving ample room for processions to move between them.

I found a seat on the aisle, and struggled to attend to the service even as I anxiously awaited confession. I didn't have to struggle for long. Early in the service, the guestmaster tapped my shoulder from behind, and signaled for me to follow him.

He led me to the entry of a small chapel to the left of the central nave, and told me Father Gregory was inside.

He was. A tall, surprisingly young-looking monk of, I'd guess, around forty-something stood waiting by two chairs near the icon of Christ. I kissed his hand saying, "*Evlogeíte.*"

He blessed me, saying, "*O, Kyrios!*" and indicated that I should take a seat. In slightly Greek-inflected English, he asked me to begin.

Here, I thought, was my chance finally to take care of some old business. I told him that there were sins in my past that, because I hadn't named them specifically in confession before, continued to burden my conscience.

He asked why I hadn't named them in confession before this, and I answered that my priest—my first priest, the one who had chrismated me when I became Orthodox—had always encouraged a more general confession. At the time, I had been relieved; but in the interim, memory of these past sins had, off and on, continued to eat at me.

Father Gregory said, "Listen," and met my eyes intensely with his, "the greater sin is not trusting in forgiveness." He continued, "Judas sinned when he betrayed Jesus Christ. Peter sinned when he denied Jesus Christ. Both could have been forgiven, not just Peter. The sin that destroyed Judas was refusing to believe he could be forgiven."

Hearing those words was like—as they say—a weight being lifted. Nodding, I confessed my nagging sins, and then I also confessed my doubt.

And even as I spoke of it, my doubt was also lifted.

I knelt, and Father Gregory draped his stole over my head to pray the prayers of absolution. I felt his hand of blessing touching my head in the sign of the cross, then felt him take my hand to help me to my feet.

I left almost laughing, and stood grinning in the narthex as Vespers concluded. It never fails: I walk into confession anxious; I walk out relieved. This was the first time, however, that I walked out feeling absolutely elated, knowing that for once I had also left my doubt behind.

———

On my way out to trápeza, I was met by a monk who appeared to be striding in a deliberate beeline to me from across the courtyard. As he drew near, he put out his hand to shake mine, saying in clearly American English, "Hi, I'm Father Matthew."

"I'm Isaák," I said, surprised to be so jovially met. "Where are you from?"

He was from Wisconsin, and we chatted only briefly as he led me to trápeza. As he left me at my table, he said he'd show me around later on, after the veneration of the relics.

Following our meal of garlicky orzo and squid (the wine was a soft rosé), I crossed the courtyard, entered the katholikón, and venerated the icons as I made my way to the table placed before the Royal Doors. The priest brought out half a dozen reliquaries, one at a time and showing great tenderness toward each. He handled them as one might carry a fragile infant, and kissed each reliquary before setting it down on the table's scarlet cloth. He then opened each in turn, and kissed them again.

In seconds, I was surrounded by other pilgrims as we all pressed forward to see what lay before us. From the press behind me, I felt a hand pulling at my sleeve. It was Father Matthew, drawing me aside to whisper an English translation of the priest's explanations of the relics there: among them, a large fragment of the True Cross, a length of the reed on which Christ was offered vinegar, the right hand of Saint Katherine, the skulls of Saint John Chrysostom and Saint Gregory the Theologian, and—most compelling—the miracle-working belt of the Theotokos.

Again, I offered my prayer rope to the priest so that he might bless it with the relics. Thereafter, Father Matthew took me on a personal tour of the monastery, the several miracle-working icons, and a few of the smaller chapels. Along the way, he pointed out the archeological dig going on within the monastery walls—something of a rarity, but nicely indicative of the spirit Vatopédi shares with Simonópetra, where scholarship and study are encouraged. The library, for instance, holds more than twenty-five thousand printed volumes, and more than two thousand ancient manuscripts. Like the community at Simonópetra, the monks at Vatopédi appear to be international, educated, and interested in the pilgrims who come to them—not that they would let any of those virtues deter them from their primary pursuit: becoming prayer.

As we said good night there in the courtyard before the katholikón, Father Matthew pointed out several other rarities, bits of pagan sculpture and architecture that—having been unearthed during the excavation for the katholikón—had been incorporated into the stonework of the church itself. "The point is," he said, "Christ makes all things new," even the broken bits of pagan temples.

———

Back in my room, I settled in to read further in the book Father Iákovos had given me, *The Authentic Seal* of Yéronda Aimilianós.

The yéronda proved to be a perfect companion for a quiet evening in pursuit of prayer.

In the elders word's, I recognized much of what Father Iákovos had been teaching me, in particular about the agonistic nature of prayer, for the yéronda also refers to Jacob's experience with the angel. When we finally start to pray, the yéronda writes, "we experience prayer, initially, as a wrestling match, as a struggle."

But he makes an interesting distinction that I had not yet noticed:

———

A struggle, not in the sense that it is difficult to pray, that I have to struggle to gather my thoughts and overcome my sleepiness or the weariness in my knees. . . . Not struggle in the sense that I am hungry and I want to go and eat, but I say "No, I shall continue to pray." I do not mean that struggle. That is the ascetic struggle and is something different—another thing altogether. I am not speaking of the struggle we have with ourselves, but the struggle we have with God. I wrestle with God. It is quite clear. . . . When I do not have the sense of this struggle with God, I have not even begun to pray.

———

It occurred to me, therefore, that I had not even begun to pray.

I suppose that I had suspected as much.

Just the same, I was finally beginning to gather the difference between, say, the struggle to overcome my own weaknesses—appetites, laziness, muddled thought—and the struggle to grip God, to insist—as Jacob has insisted—that He bless.

I read long into the night, poring over the troubling terms of the heavy book in my hands, leaning into the teachings of this old man who had tasted prayer and had helped his brotherhood of monks and nuns taste it as well. What I learned made me all the more eager to return to Simonópetra, and to visit further with Father Iákovos. At the very least I knew I would write to him soon; I hoped he would realize that I was writing because I must.

What I wanted to attain—besides, perhaps, a reliable, God-acquiring half nelson—was an ability to discern in prayer, as Yéronda

Aimilianós put it, "when the mouth is speaking, or the heart, or the spirit, because, in the end, it's not the heart that should speak: it's the spirit which should speak in the heart."

This grappling with God, then, turns out to be a singular means by which God's presence in the human heart is realized. It is not, finally, *my* prayer that I'm after, but *the prayer of the Holy Spirit in me praying*, praying from the restored, noetic center of my person, my one-day recovered *nous* connecting me to Christ *and*, as it happens, His existential Body, the Church.

I read until my eyes burned, then spoke my prayers, and lay down to sleep.

Instead of sleeping, I struggled. With my hands pressed hard against my chest, I prayed the Jesus Prayer and labored to get a grip on God, but felt as if He wasn't giving in. That's when things seemed to get tougher, but the tálanton rang out soon thereafter to let me off the hook. I threw cold tap water on my face and hurried through cold rain across the courtyard to the katholikón, having not slept a wink.

———

Once again, I was one of the first to arrive. A single monk stood reading prayers at a chanter's stand in the exonarthex; a single oil lamp near him offered the only light. In that suddenly oppressive gloom, I kept at the prayer, feeling pretty much alone—feeling, frankly, lost.

I recognized the moment as one of the apparently barren times. The elation I'd known after confession seemed like a sensation from another life, and I hunkered in a wooden stall near the icon of the Theotokos, puzzling over this sudden turn. I felt a little angry, even. I felt as if I were slipping.

And with that thought—my having slipped into melancholy—I recalled a favorite saying of Saint Isaak: "Let us not grieve when we make a slip, but when we become hardened by it." I had, admittedly, lost some ground when I realized during my vigil of reading how little ground I had gained to begin with. That realization—and my willingness to give in to the melodrama of self-pity—now threatened to do more damage yet, to harden me, even, against the possibility of future progress.

At the conclusion of the midnight prayers, I entered the nave, took my place in a likely stall, forgave myself, and—in the midst of savoring a beautiful orthros and Divine Liturgy—found my way back to life.

More accurately, I found my way back to the *way of life*, the journey on which—it suddenly occurred to me—every juncture appears to be but another beginning.

12

This sickness is not unto death.

Father Matthew caught up with me after trápeza to say good-bye. I was tempted to tell him a little about my night, my reading, my surprise attack of melancholy, but we spoke mostly about my plans to return in the spring. He gave me his e-mail address, which, under the circumstances, seemed a comic curiosity.

Few of the monasteries are "wired" to the Internet, and those few are very careful with access. I was probably a little slow to catch on, but realized that the kind and thoughtful Father Matthew enjoys certain duties and privileges having to do with the procurement of useful items that are not readily available on the Holy Mountain. To that end, he asked if I might send along an electronics catalog when I had the chance. I said I would.

I hurried back to my room to pack up, then rushed to the gate to meet the microbus. I would ride to Karyés, then board the bus for Dáfni, then take the late boat to Xenofóndos, where Father Zakarías was expecting me.

———

By the time I made it to the boat, the weather had taken a very nasty turn. Whitecaps virtually covered the surface of the sea. The boat sat rocking in its ropes so violently that the crew decided not even to attempt loading the dump truck that had been idling at the pier. The driver parked the truck and scrambled on board with the rest of us. Had I been thinking clearly, I probably would have kept going, stayed on the boat until Ouranoúpoli, making certain I'd get to Thessaloníki in time for my flight.

Well, maybe I wasn't thinking clearly. At the very least, I wasn't thinking clearly by conventional standards. All the way to Xenofóndos,

I played the options over in my mind. I could disembark, visit with Father Zakarías, taste life at yet another monastery, or I could stay on the boat and spend the night in Ouranoúpoli, arriving in Thessaloníki a couple days earlier than I'd planned. If I disembarked, however, I would also be able to travel to Grigoríou one more time, as I'd promised Father Cosmás, to celebrate the vigil and the Feast of Saint Nicholas.

———

Then a strange thing happened. As the boat churned through huge swells and squalls, I started thinking about food. Ten days living like a monk poses a number of challenges for the dilettante pilgrim, not the least of which is hunger, genuine hunger, of the sort that makes your knees tremble as you walk, your head throb as you pray. We're given plenty to eat, really, but it's all so doggone healthy—no meat at all, little fish, and on a good many days not even any oil or cheese. On top of that, I had been doing quite a bit of hiking on this trip—more, even, than I had in the summertime, and I'd generally slept no more than five hours each night, most often less. I was thinking *enough is enough*. Weariness of body and weariness of soul, at that moment, conspired to keep me on the boat; I was already thinking of the lamb chops and tzatziki waiting for me in Ouranoúpoli.

And then an even stranger thing happened.

I suddenly felt ashamed for putting such things ahead of my continuing need (and, it fairly seemed, my *increasing* need) for prayer. No sooner had I realized what was *really* luring me away, I put it aside, and, when soon thereafter the boat pulled away from Xenofóndos, I was already halfway to the monastery gate. Maybe I wasn't so good at wrestling with God, but the struggle with myself was a breeze—the guy's a wimp.

—— *Xenofóndos Monastery* ——

Xenofóndos is stunningly beautiful, and apparently thriving. The monastery's restoration seems all but complete, though new construction is well underway for, significantly, a new wing of monastic cells. The original katholikón—near the guesthouse, the trápeza, and adjacent chapels dedicated to Saint Demetrios and Saint Lazarus, respectively—dates from the eleventh century and continues to be used; a newer, exceedingly spacious katholikón (the largest among the ruling monasteries, and second in size only to the enormous kyriakón at Saint Andrew's Skete) has been erected in the center of the compound, near the bell tower. Its expansive narthex, marble iconostasis, and inlaid marble floor are the most beautiful I have seen. The guesthouse (reminiscent of the one at Vatopédi) appears very like a well designed *pension*; and I was astonished to learn that the monastery is equipped to offer hospitality to as many as two thousand visitors at a time. My room on the second floor overlooked the arsanás, where the sea seemed to have calmed a bit. Waves continued to splash over the concrete pier, but less violently.

Once I'd settled in, I asked the guestmaster about Father Zakarías. He led me to the ground floor of the bell tower, where we found the young monk busy at his task of preparing wooden boards for the iconographers at work in the tower above. He welcomed me with a warm embrace and the offer of hot tea; I accepted both gladly.

During our visit, he led me up the bell tower's staircase to see the state-of-the-art iconography studios above. A good many monasteries and sketes support their existence with the production of icons, and, admittedly, *any* icon manifests beauty, offers a sense of the intersection of visible and invisible presence. Even so, the level of accomplishment— the craft and artistry manifested by the icons at Xenofóndos—spoke to yet another level of discipline and devotion. From the preparation of the carefully selected wooden boards on the ground floor to the final buffing of the golden inlay on the fourth floor—and clearly at every laborious step along the way—the loving attention paid to each image-in-the-making was unmistakably superior. These were among the most beautiful and most powerfully affecting icons I have ever seen.

———

Not surprisingly, following our visit, Vespers was sweet as ever, resounding with particular brightness in the marbled vault of the spacious katholikón. After trápeza, Father Zakarías walked me to the guesthouse for conversation and coffee. He had first come to Athos as a seminary student whose professors had encouraged him to make a pilgrimage to Mount Athos before the duties of parish life and family life would make such a journey more difficult to arrange, less likely to happen.

Evidently, that one trip was all it took for Father Zakarías; he never returned to the States. We spoke late into the evening, and in his calm and quiet voice—telling me his story, showing genuine interest in mine—he helped me to recognize what stillness looked like from the outside. His conversation was woven with the writings of the Fathers, whose words he had long since internalized, and made his own.

———

I was awake—and quite suddenly—well before the call of the tálanton. I went to the balcony of the guesthouse to begin my prayer. The air was still quite crisp, but the wind had let up overnight and the sky had cleared. Countless stars filled the sky, and their countless reflections streaked the sea, which continued to swell.

In the midst of my prayer, I had a delicious sense—oddly concurrent—of both God's enormity and His absolute nearness. I suppose I might have said that I stopped praying at that point; more truly, I think, I found myself more deeply *in prayer*, and therefore speechless.

I'm not sure how long this lasted, but I was drawn out of that moment by the familiar clatter of the tálanton, and made my way across the monastery grounds to the katholikón.

This odd sensation—was it a sinking beneath the language of prayer? a descent to the heart? a taste of stillness?—returned to me throughout the midnight service, orthros, and notably during the Great Entrance of the liturgy itself.

When I received the Holy Mysteries, I came upon a new and powerful apprehension, as if at the tongue something in me were meeting with itself.

Forgive the cliché, but I tasted, and I saw.

I don't suppose I can say this any more clearly, though I'm guessing that what I'm writing now is of scant help. This will have to do: there is a moment when petition is eclipsed by presence, and that is as close as I have come, so far, to the prayer I've been seeking.

———

Right after the Divine Liturgy, I said my good-byes to Father Zakarías, thanking him for his hospitality; I skipped trápeza in order to catch the early boat back to Dáfni. I was able to score a coffee and a toast on board, then sat on the open deck to enjoy the rocking cruise. The weather had settled a bit during the previous twenty-four hours, and I was grateful that I could spend my last nights on Athos celebrating the vigil and the Feast of Saint Nicholas at Grigoríou.

Father Cosmás greeted me with another pot of American-style coffee, eager to hear how my journey had gone. Robin Amis was also still there, and I was treated to a sneak peek of their nearly complete translation of Abbot George's book on théosis.

As I read, I kept thinking that my experience during Communion at Xenofóndos had occasioned a new sense of much of what met me on the printed page, there in the archondaríki kitchen. For one, I had a renewed sense that the animating life within us, by appalling grace, is mystically congruent with the very Life we receive, partaking of the cup.

A great many scattered apprehensions and apparently serendipitous experiences seemed to be coming together now at the end of my second pilgrimage. I found myself taking care not to make too much of their convergence. On the one hand, I was pleased to think that God had actually led me here, and that He was actively showing me something I needed to see; on the other hand, I was wary of the hubris involved in imagining such immediate direction.

It would have been handy to have had, say, a spiritual father help me sort it out.

In any case, the monastery was bustling in preparation for the vigil and the feast. As I mentioned, the general rule is that no one is to be turned away from a monastery's festal celebrations, and the fathers were expecting somewhere in the neighborhood of four hundred pilgrims for the weekend.

In the midst of these many preparations, the sky went black by mid-afternoon. The weather turned from rough to violent within the space of about fifteen minutes. From the northern headland, a small speedboat, the *Sophia*, came bounding over the waves to deliver a somewhat shaken bishop and his entourage from Thessaloníki; the bishop would be presiding over the vigil.

His would be the last arrival, save for a handful of monks hiking in from Saint Paul's and Dionysíou.

The expected hundreds of pilgrims were probably languishing in Ouranoúpoli or already returning home, having been unable to board the *Áxion Estín*, which had suspended its service.

This was the first time it occurred to me that I might have trouble getting home; still, I wasn't overly concerned, given that I had a good two and a half days until my morning flight from Thessaloniki. Father Cosmás adopted a nearly comic disposition toward the matter, saying with a big smile that the boats were suspended for two weeks about this time last year, and saying that, if the boats were never to run again, I'd be welcome to become a monk. "I'm sure your wife will understand," he said, grinning.

In the meantime, the dearth of guests freed Father Cosmás from a good number of duties he otherwise would have had to undertake, and we took advantage of this gift of time to talk; he also showed me around the monastery.

The most memorable part of my tour was the cemetery and the cemetery chapel, just outside the southernmost gate, and poised on a narrow terrace between the steep slope above the monastery and the sheer cliff (maybe a two-hundred-foot vertical drop) upon which the monastery is built. He showed me the chapel, pointing out some of the unusual frescos of the narthex and the close quarters of the nave and altar space. This is the chapel where, I gathered, Father Cosmás most often celebrates the liturgy with a handful of his brothers. When we'd ducked our heads to exit the tight doorway, we stood at the cliff edge, looking out at that amazing sea for a good ten minutes in silence. As I was turning to head back toward the katholikón and the refectory, Father Cosmás asked if I'd yet seen the ossuary. I had not.

Observed from the outside, the Orthodox manner with the dead— which is, as it happens, the early Church's manner—can seem a little strange. For starters, the dead are unlikely to be spoken of as dead. They are *asleep*. Since the resurrection of Christ, the Christian person does not die, per se. He falls asleep. He is said to have fallen asleep "*in* the Lord."

Let that curious *in* trouble the air for a moment.

On Mount Athos, when the monk falls asleep, he is buried—as most Orthodox are buried wherever the laws of the land allow it—unembalmed.

One other curiosity to note: rigor mortis does not happen on Mount Athos. You may think I'm kidding. I am not. You're wondering why such an apparently trivial matter is of consequence. I wonder the same thing. For whatever reason—and I can think of nary a one—when these monks fall asleep, their bodies remain from deathbed to wooden coffin to tiny cemetery plot, pliant and weighty—as if they *were* simply asleep. Father Cosmás apprehends this phenomenon as a gift to the monks, a special gift from a loving God.

But back to the general practice. The first Orthodox funeral I ever attended was at Holy Trinity Church in Santa Fe, New Mexico. Just down the road from Saint John's College, where I, off and on, take part in the Glen/Image Workshops that meet there every summer. I showed up at Holy Trinity for Sunday liturgy with my friend Warren Farha, an Antiochian Orthodox brother from Wichita and the proprietor of the incomparable bookstore, Eighth Day Books. On that morning, we were met by a simple, pine coffin as soon as we stepped inside the nave.

Like a good many Orthodox churches, this church was without pews or chairs. In such cases, parishioners generally stand for the duration of the services, though chairs are available for the elderly, the infirm, and small children. When the homily rolls around, some folks take the opportunity to sit or hunker on the floor, especially if the pastor tends to wax (let's say) toward the windy.

On this morning, the parishioners stood around a wooden coffin resting on three sawhorses in the very center of the sanctuary. The coffin was open, and lying prominently among that community of the faithful was an elderly man—asleep.

I was initially startled, then strangely moved.

Whereas popular culture has, for the most part, removed death and dying far from view—nudging death itself to the very periphery of collective consciousness—here was a practice insisting that the phenomenon be given center stage. Throughout the liturgy that followed, family and friends continued to worship by his side. Children and adults both turned to him throughout the service, as if to see if he was comfortable, attending to him as if he were still present.

And, frankly, he was.

During the Communion hymn, one slight girl with straight dark hair reached up and laid her right hand upon his two hands—pale, cold, and crossed upon his chest. She held his hands like that until it was her turn to approach the cup.

———

When my own father died, we missed out on most of this. Following a nearly forty-eight-hour vigil in his hospital room—during most of which he had struggled to breathe, nearly panting in his efforts—it was with some relief that we watched him take his last few breaths—made easier by morphine—and settle into . . . sleep. We wept, of course, but we had little in our experience to help us to attend as fully to his body— attend to *him*—as we might have, or as, perhaps, we should have. I've written about this experience before, in a poem called "Regarding the Body":

I too was a decade coming to terms
with how abruptly my father had died.
And still I'm lying about it. His death
was surely as incremental, slow-paced
as any, and certainly as any
I had witnessed. Still, as we met around him
that last morning—none of us unaware
of what the morning would bring—I was struck
by how quickly he left us. And the room
emptied—comes to me now—far too quickly.
If impiety toward the dead were still
deemed sin, it was that morning our common
trespass, to have imagined too readily
his absence, to have all but denied him
as he lay, simply, present before us.

What comes to me *now* is that—in our turning away so soon afterward—we missed something both precious and sustaining; this *something* is what the folks at Holy Trinity in Santa Fe did not miss, and something that the monks of Mount Athos are also very careful to retain.

Father Cosmás pulled a key from his pocket and led the way down three narrow steps leading beneath ground level to a wooden door in the stone foundation of the cemetery chapel. He pushed that door open, and invited me to enter. There was hardly room for the two of us, stooping beneath the low ceiling, for the space was all but taken up with bins of stacked bones and rows lined with skulls.

Vertigo was immediate, and powerful. I had to place my hand on the low ceiling to keep from falling over. I recognized the large bucket at my feet—the one that had held bones earlier in the year when I was returning to Grigoríou along the trail here. Those bones had been the remains of a monk who had fallen asleep some three years before, and whose bones had on that day been retrieved from the small cemetery plot. His empty grave, in the meantime, had been used to inter another father who had fallen asleep.

Father Cosmás waited with me, without saying a word, letting the "memory of death" do its efficacious work.

Back outside, we stood awhile longer at the edge of the cliff; the sea had become wild.

———

I would remain at Grigoríou for two nights. The first was taken up with the festal vigil. The second was something of a private vigil, as I barely slept, keeping my eyes on the sea, praying that it would settle enough to allow the boats to run. If I didn't catch the boat in the morning—or, at the very least, catch the last boat of the afternoon—I would not make it to Thessaloníki in time for my flight. It was, moreover, the week before Christmas, and the odds that I would get a seat on any subsequent flight were pretty slim.

Father Cosmás knocked on my door before the tálanton, and told me he had heard that the *Ágia Ánna* would certainly not be coming to the Grigoríou dock that morning; there was a chance, however—albeit a slight one—that the *Áxion Estín* would make it as far as Dáfni. He suggested that I hike to Simonópetra, then walk the road to Dáfni. If I left by 7:00 AM, he said, I might catch Father Iákovos between liturgy and trápeza, to learn if he had any ideas about getting me home. The tálanton sounded out, and Father Cosmás left to prepare for the service. I finished packing and hurried to the katholikón.

At the end of orthros, I venerated the icons one last time, and slipped out before liturgy to begin my climb to Simonópetra. The rain was only intermittent, but my clothes were soaked through, and I was gasping for breath—my legs burning—when I hobbled into the courtyard forty minutes later. I believe I set a record for climbing that particular stretch of trail.

The fathers were still in services when I finally collapsed in the archondaríki, but one of the younger monks happened by, recognizing me and asking, "Isaák, where did you come from?"

I told him about my situation, and he told me how doubtful it was that the boats would be running, even as far a Dáfni. I suggested that maybe I'd try walking to Ouranoúpoli, which he first took to be a joke, then—I gathered from his suddenly puzzled scowl—took to be a sign of my foolishness. "No, not possible," he said. "I'll find Father Iákovos."

I was not the only one potentially stranded for the moment, though I might have been the only one who would be missing a plane as a result. When Father Iákovos arrived in the archondaríki, he was accompanied by two men from Thessaloníki, longtime friends of the monastery, Stelios Zarganes and Argyris Doumas. They, too, needed to get home, if possible, that day. For one, Argyris—whose nuclear medicine clinic is the busiest in the city—had many patients waiting for his return.

Long story short: Father Iákovos and Father Metrophánes made many phone calls in an attempt to find us a way to Ouranoúpoli, but even the chartered taxi boats weren't running. The fathers, however, did arrange to have us driven to Dáfni in the monastery Land Rover.

As I prepared to go, Father Iákovos returned from his cell with a final gift: a large icon of Saint Isaak of Syria, my name-saint. "Do you think you have room in your pack for this?" he asked.

We embraced, and he whispered, "I'll be praying, Isaak. Don't be anxious. See what comes."

―――――

When we arrived in Dáfni, I was astonished to see the crowd of men—well over five hundred of them—languishing at the pier. Most seemed fairly content with the situation, but a few were already showing some of the anxiety I was feeling, rushing about, raising their voices in anger, shouting at the dockworkers as if it were their fault the boats weren't running.

I have to admit that, for the previous twelve hours, I had managed to let that very anxiety erode most of the stillness I had cultivated during these two weeks on the Holy Mountain. It was as if a switch had been thrown in the back of my brain, effectively delivering me right back into the world of the minute hand; it had been, for a good twelve hours, as if I hadn't learned a thing.

I suddenly remembered—and wrote in my journal that very minute—something W. H. Auden had observed: *The opposite of faith is not doubt, but anxiety.*

I did my best to flip back the switch.

As the hours dragged on, I found my way back—as the Zen monk Sohsen might have said—to *being here, now*; also, I did what Father Iákovos had suggested, waiting to see what would come.

A good bit did come, but nary a boat. I met several folks there at the pier, shared food and wine with a group of young men who'd set up camp in the café patio, and was blessed by an elder who happened by. I managed to find a cozy corner of the patio that was out of the wind, and settled in to read. I pulled Yéronda Aimelianós's book from my pack, and leaned into it.

―――――

The next fourteen hours passed in an intensely introspective cycle. I would read for a while, get up to stretch my legs, browse through the few shops there at the landing, stand at the edge of the concrete pier, pray the prayer, and return to my corner and to my book. I seemed to be in silent conversation the entire time; even when I was in actual conversation with another pilgrim or a monk, I was conscious that God was very near, listening. I tried very hard to listen back.

At one point, I was able to reach my wife, Marcia, by card telephone to tell her that I would certainly be missing my plane. I asked her to get hold of our travel agent, the excellent Barbara Davis, to see if she could get me on a subsequent flight. I wouldn't know until the next afternoon if she'd been able to do so.

As afternoon dimmed and darkened to evening, most of the crowd dispersed by bus, microbus, and Land Rover to monasteries and sketes where they had found—or hoped to find—shelter. I was loathe to flip that particular switch, engaging the anxious mode once again. I took a deep breath, looked around, and decided that the covered patio of the tavern was as good a place as any to spend the night. By 9:00 PM, I had—I thought—settled in for a night of reading and praying. At about 10:00 PM, the power generator was shut off, and the patio went black; I dug into my pack for the bundle of beeswax tapers I'd packed for home. With an empty beer bottle as my candle stand, I lit a candle, and kept reading.

There were still a hundred or so men hunkered down in pockets around the landing. Conversation and occasional singing could be heard from all corners of the darkened port. Off and on, what I took to be a punch line would be nearly shouted, followed by hoots of laughter.

About midnight, I was surprised to hear a voice call out from the darkness, "*Isaák? Íste edthó?*"—"Isaák? You're here?" It was Argyris. He and Stelios had found beds in one of the buildings that Simonópetra maintains at Dáfni. Their friend, the port supervisor, Father Metrophánes, had taken them in.

Argyris was chagrined that I hadn't gone up to one of the monasteries, and was insistent that I not stay where I was. "You'll freeze," he said. He had been taking a walk with Florín, one of the many Romanian laborers working for Simonópetra at Dáfni; and now I could hear him in conversation with Florín. I gathered that they were talking about me.

Florín was nodding as Argyris turned back to me and announced, "Florín has a place for you."

The place that Florín had was his own. I followed my two rescuers across the darkened port to a ramshackle, two-story building at the back of the port complex. We climbed to the second floor to the small room that Florin shared with another Romanian worker. I could see that he was pulling his things off the larger bed and putting them on a bare mattress on the upper level of a bunk bed across the room. Clearly, he was giving me his own bed.

I saw that the only thing I could do was to accept the kindness. He offered me food, and coffee. When we had eaten, he pulled a two-liter bottle of tsípouro from the cupboard.

And thus we spent an interesting night, sharing pictures of our families, sharing a good portion of that bottle, and trading words in Greek, Romanian, and English. We laughed a lot, though I wasn't always sure exactly why.

Around 2:00 AM, Florin left for a while, coming back to report what I took, initially, to be a surprising invitation to get out of his apartment. "Tomorrow, boat come. Tomorrow, boat no come. You go!"

"*Ne,*" I said. "*Avrio,* I go."

"*Avrio,*" he said, "boat come, no come, you go. Speedboat."

"OK," I said, starting to get it. "What speedboat?"

"*Sophia,* you go *Sophia.*"

Over the course of the next hour, amid several more rounds of tsípouro, the plan began to take dim shape in my mind. Father Metrophánes had made certain that Stelios, Argyris, and I would have seats on the *Sophia,* the only boat guaranteed to be running in the morning. All I had to do was be sure to show up at the pier by 8:00 AM.

I was relieved that I'd be getting to Ouranoúpoli in the morning, but was far more relieved to realize Florín hadn't been telling me I wasn't welcome. We pretty much polished off the tsípouro, and called it a night.

When I woke up, I was alone in the apartment. A mug of lukewarm coffee sat next to me on the bed table. I drank it down, and hurried to the pier dragging my pack. The crowd was back to its full complement, probably five hundred men, all of whom appeared to be in a pretty bad mood, anxious to learn about the boats.

Argyris and Stelios found me immediately. "We were looking for you, Isaák!"

They had already bought my ticket, and refused to let me pay them back. Quite surprisingly, Stelios expressed "embarrassment" that they hadn't been able to take better care of me the day before. This baffled me at first, but as I got to know him better, I realized that, for Stelios, hospitality is quite a serious matter, both a duty and a joy.

When the *Sophia* arrived at the dock, the crowd appeared very like a mob, with a good third of the five hundred men pressing to buy their way aboard. The uniformed customs agents were able to escort the forty men with tickets—our trio included—to the boat without incident.

Once we were underway, Stelios came to where I was sitting and asked how I was getting to Thessaloníki. I told him I would take the bus. "No, you won't," he said, turning back to his seat.

The trip that would have taken us two hours on the *Áxion Estín* was accomplished in about forty minutes. We disembarked at the pier, and my new friends showed me the way to Stelios's car. We drove the "quick way" back (taking a little less than two hours) and drove Argyris directly to his clinic, where his patients eagerly awaited their cancer treatments.

On the way to my hotel, Stelios asked if I wouldn't rather come stay with him and his family. Had I not been as filthy as I was—two weeks without hot water, and two days without so much as a cold Athonite shower—I would have accepted; as it was, I told Stelios that I'd need a good hot bath before anyone should let me anywhere near his house *or* his family. He laughed, but insisted that he pick me up later for dinner.

So, that was how—once I had to let go of my own, failed plans—the Body of Christ took up the slack. In the evening, Stelios fetched me at the curb across from my hotel, and took me to his home, where I met his wife—Sophia, as it happens—and their son Tryfon. They fed me, gave me drink, shared their stories with me, attended with great interest to my own meandering story, and sent me home loaded with gifts for my family and even for our young Orthodox parish back home.

My new rule, based upon what Father Iákovos had encouraged: whenever things go wrong, wait and see what better thing is coming.

Meanwhile, the excellent Barbara Davis had gotten me a seat on the morning flight, as well as timely connections all the way to St. Louis. I was home about twenty-four hours later.

13

not without honor, save in his own country.

I had pretty much decided as early as September that, sooner than later, I'd be making a trip to Saint Anthony's Monastery in Arizona. The oddness of my first day on Mount Athos—exacerbated by a complex mix of tragedy and elation—had been punctuated late in the evening by the two casual questions I had received from Father Iosíf. He had asked if I had been to Saint Anthony's Monastery, and he'd asked if I had sought out Elder Ephrém, the man who had been Philothéou's abbot for many years before leaving the Holy Mountain to establish monasteries in America.

No and *no* had been my answers.

An exceedingly puzzled look had been his response.

His perplexity, as I have come to understand it, had to do with wondering why I would travel more than five thousand miles in search of a guide into the prayer of the heart when one of the elders of Mount Athos lived (with several other Athonite fathers) less than a thousand miles away from my home in Missouri.

To which I would have to say I am not exactly sure.

———

Beyond that, over the intervening months, the memory of Father Iosíf's puzzlement has led me to puzzle over another perplexity: Why had my hunger for the fullness of the faith and my desire for genuine prayer taken me so far from the church I had loved as a child, so far from the community that had sparked my desire for God in the first place?

I'm still mulling that one over, too. I can say only that my increasing hunger for worship and for prayer had drawn me toward the East, as my hunger would not be satisfied with what had become very thin soup.

In any event, I felt then that I should set out to see what I might see—
to learn what I might *taste and see*—in a monastic community closer
to home. Therefore, after my second pilgrimage to Mount Athos, I set
out for the Monastery of Saint Anthony in Arizona. On the Thursday
of Bright Week (the week following Holy Pascha—or Easter, to most
folks), I landed in Phoenix late in the evening, picked up my rental car,
and headed southeast to Florence. Father Markéllos, the guestmaster
and apparent bookstore manager, had instructed me through a phone
call to Seraphima that if I didn't get to the monastery by 8:00 PM, I
should wait until 12:30 AM to enter. The monks would be unavailable
in the meantime, and my arrival within that space of time would mean
someone would have to depart from his routine—perhaps, even, his
prayer rule—to tend to me.

That would be a bad thing.

So, as I surely would not be able to arrive before 8:00 PM, I had
planned to arrive sometime around 10:00, and to sit reading in the car
until 12:30 AM. As it happened, I didn't need to wait that long at all, not
in the monastery parking lot anyway.

On my drive to the monastery, I happened upon a burning bush.

Well, several of them.

A whole desert of burning bushes.

A wildfire had broken out the day before, and I ended up doing
most of my waiting behind a roadblock about six miles shy of the
monastery gate. By the time the Forest Service called an "all clear,"
it was nearly midnight, and I rolled into the gravel parking lot about
fifteen minutes later.

Along the way, I had driven through a mile or so of burning
grasses, mesquite, and saguaro cacti. In particular, one huge mesquite
bush about fifteen feet high—less than five feet off the road—was fully
engulfed in flame as I drove past it—my own burning bush in the
desert. I didn't hear any voices, but I may have been getting something
of a message, even so.

Minutes later, I sat in my parked car, gazing at the brilliant night
sky bursting with stars, and gazing to the north, where the horizon

glowed red from the wildfire. At the far end of the expansive gravel lot, three Forest Service fire trucks and their attendant crews were holding the line against any flare-ups that might send the fire our direction. I could see their silhouettes—the trucks as well as the men themselves—vividly magnified before a backdrop of red glow. As I watched the surreal scene, I tried to refocus on why I had come.

To say the least, my search for a spiritual father had not gone exactly as planned. Early in my year of pilgrimage, I had supposed that I would find a likely elder on my first visit to the Holy Mountain—maybe even *early* in that visit—and that I would be able to make two subsequent trips to seek his continuing guidance regarding prayer. As it turned out, two journeys to Mount Athos had already come and gone, and as far as I could tell I had yet to find that father.

Along the way, that particular disappointment had led to my supposing that perhaps what I'd been seeking in Greece may have been waiting all along, much closer to home. I would be at Saint Anthony's for an entire week, and I hoped to meet both Yéronda Ephrém, the elder, and Yéronda Paísios, the abbot. Both men hear confessions at the monastery, and each serves as spiritual father to the community of monks and to the many pilgrims who arrive there every day.

I hunkered in the car, and said the prayer. I recalled a particular saying of the monks, made in response to any request of their elders, as well as to any overt expression of their own hearts: "May it be blessed."

That's what I said as I stepped out of the car and onto the gravel lot; that's what I kept repeating as my crunching steps took me to the gate.

Soon as I'd passed through, I was in the waiting area—a terra cotta sandstone patio with a large and elegant gazebo structure—immediately to the left of the entryway. Just beyond the gazebo stood the bookstore building where I'd been told to meet Father Markéllos. Even in the moonlight, I could see that the monastery was a lush oasis, with garden after garden stretching far into the night. At that moment, a light went on inside the cell beside the bookstore, and I saw that my host was on his way to meet me. A small monk opened the door and stepped out. He saw me standing there in the dark, and asked if I was Isaák.

This was *not*, I learned, Father Markéllos, but was, rather, the surprisingly young—in his early twenties, maybe—Father Nicódemos; he welcomed me with almost painful shyness, and asked me to follow him to the guesthouse. He led me without another word; rather, he led me saying what I took to be the Jesus Prayer—albeit in Greek—under his breath, punctuated like a cadence beginning with an audible *Kyrie*. The sandstone path wound through an expanse of palm trees, flowering trees, and cacti, leading to the men's guesthouse.

Once inside, Father Nicódemos showed me to my room, and told me that the midnight service would begin at 3:30. Then he made a beeline for the door, still whispering the prayer.

———

I would spend my week at Saint Anthony's worshiping for the most part in the central katholikón (dedicated to Saints Anthony and Nektarios), but also in Saint George's Church, in Saint Nicholas's Church, and praying alone in Saint Demetrios's Chapel. I was also able to venerate relics in a small chapel dedicated to Saint Panteleímon the Healer. Other chapels on the grounds are dedicated to Saint Seraphim of Sarov and to Saint John the Baptist. The place is immense, and apparently growing, with every detail of construction undertaken with utmost care.

The monastery was first established in 1995, when Yéronda Ephrém, the abbot of Philothéou on the Holy Mountain, sent six Athonite monks to land that the monastery had acquired in the Sonoran Desert of Arizona. Prior to this, Yéronda Ephrém had led in the repopulation and restoration of no fewer than four monasteries on the Holy Mountain, as well as several women's monasteries in mainland Greece. He had visited Canada and the United States in 1979, and was moved to action by a perceived lack of monastic support for Orthodox Christians of North America.

Those six monks set immediately to work, drilling a well, and building the katholikón, the living space for the monks, the trápeza, and guesthouses for men and women. With water from a very deep but surprisingly munificent well, they began irrigating their little corner of the desert, developing a veritable oasis with extensive vegetable gardens, a vineyard, citrus orchards, and an olive grove. Today, the many churches, chapels, and the array of wooden and stone structures are all connected by an elaborate system of gardens, pathways, and pergolas with Mediterranean fountains. I would walk the entirety of the grounds during my week there, never quite managing to get my mind around the reach of the monastery's lush expanse. It was evident, even so, that further construction is still underway; the trápeza was being enlarged, nearly doubling its size; newer fountains and chapels on the periphery and new sandstone and slate paths signaled that the vision continues, extends.

The brotherhood at Saint Anthony's now exceeds forty monks. There is also a community of nuns living nearby, under the protection of the monastery and served by its priests and elders. During the week I was there—a relatively slow week by local standards—there were easily fifty pilgrims on any given day as well. The monks range in age from the late teens to, I'd guess, men in their sixties. Elder Ephrém himself was then nearly eighty, but the majority of the fathers seemed to be relatively young men, with a surprising many in their twenties. This strikes me, alternately, as a remarkable tribute and a remarkable weirdness. That a good dozen men in their late teens and early twenties have already and so definitively turned away from their culture's commonplace self-indulgence in favor of ascesis is stunning however you slice it. Some critics—including the parents of certain of these same young men—feel it to be an excess, a perversion; others recognize it as a laudable decision to pursue théosis, regardless of how such a choice may appear to those on the outside.

During my week there, I was able to work side by side with a good many of these young monks—three in particular—and I was struck by how happy, how full of joy, they were. I washed and dried dishes with Father Pródromos; I set and cleared the tables in trápeza with Father Eliséios, and I dug irrigation ditches with Father Nicephoros. These young men all seemed genuinely to savor their lives of obedience and prayer. I was especially moved by the sweet contentment and a powerful sense of calm presence that were manifested by Father Nicephoros—a thin, wiry, young man who, I'm pretty sure, couldn't have been more than twenty-two, and who couldn't have seemed more at home with his vocation.

We spent three hot afternoons digging ditches and replacing irrigation junctions; he was unfailingly thoughtful, articulate, and cheerful. Off and on, through the grove of lemon trees, I'd hear him chuckling to himself as he dug, and I'd often hear through the leaves a quiet "*Doxa to Theo.*" Praise the God.

———

On the other hand, my week at Saint Anthony's was recurrently troubled by another, unfortunately familiar phenomenon that stood in stark contrast to the spirit manifested by the monks themselves. Since its founding, the monastery has attracted a surrounding community of what I would call *dour* Orthodox families, many of them converts to Orthodoxy. For several miles along the main road leading to Saint Anthony's, something of a building boom is evident. There are, perhaps, forty or so new houses built on or near monastery land.

The part that troubles me is very hard to talk about, and perhaps it is impossible to talk about without falling into sin myself. I suppose, therefore, that I may as well sin boldly, if only in hopes of clarifying what I suspect to be a somewhat debilitating disposition, and one that might distract others from the essential joy that lies at the heart of the faith.

Sometimes I think there are *two* Orthodoxies (as, perhaps, there are two Christianities)—the mystical faith of those who glimpse how little we know (and are drawn and driven by love), and the cranky faith of those who appear to know everything already (and wish the rest of us would either agree with them or disappear).

To be sure, there is no shortage of proposition offered by the Orthodox Church, in particular those propositions pronounced in the Nicene Creed, and in the conciliar canons of the Church. That said, within the church (and *now* I mean throughout both Orthodoxy and non-Orthodox Christendom), one is likely to come across two vividly distinct understandings of those propositions; the two understandings are so different that one might wonder if the diverse members actually *are* of one body, or if these differences reveal separate religions practiced by people sitting or standing side by side in worship.

How one understands these propositions (as well as how one understands the status of the Scripture from which most proposition and practice spring) pretty much sorts out the faithful into their respective camps. Some receive these propositions and paraphrases as dynamic, inexhaustible, provisional glimpses along an endless path; others grasp them as static, comprehensive, and conclusive. Some would hold that these propositions enable the beginning of our journey to meaning, while others see them as fixed certainties marking the journey's end.

The generous (and, I think, the correct) view is not confined to Orthodoxy. John Calvin wrote of Scripture that in it "God stammers with us as a nursemaid with a child." Karl Barth insisted that we understand Scripture as "the witness to the Revelation," and that we realize that Christ Himself—in all His infinite and indefinable glory— *is* the Revelation.

Saint Isaak of Syria says it like this: "Holy Scripture says many things through allegory and often employs figurative language. . . . Do not approach the words of the mysteries contained in the divine Scriptures without prayer, beseeching God for help; rather, say: Lord, grant me to perceive the power in them!"

In each of these, one apprehends the writer's sense of the Enormity beyond the paraphrase, his sense of a Truth that cannot be circumscribed, much less merely *scribed*, or—as it often seems to me— reduced to neat paraphrase.

There appear to be, as well, two distinct expressions of piety, and both are abundantly available throughout Christendom; Orthodoxy is not spared this dichotomy. One flavor of piety is manifested by monks like Fathers Nicephoros, Cosmás, and Iákovos, men who undergo even the most strenuous ascesis smiling. The other flavor is manifested by the pilgrim I called "the sheriff" at Great Lavra, the curious soul who shooshed us and rapped the knuckles of my friend who had reached across the table for an olive. The first sort privileges, I'd say, the Resurrection; the second sort privileges the Crucifixion. The first manifests gladness in all things; the second affects a severe and suffering visage. The first seems to be moving *toward* something; the second seems, primarily, to be running *from* something.

Not to put too fine a point on it: the first appears to enjoy, already, the kingdom of heaven; the second, to suffer, already, a species of hell.

———

My sense of the demographic constituting the community of Saint Anthony's was that while the monks were manifestly of the first sort, certain of the more visible local folk may have tended toward the second. My own continuing struggle during that week of services was to keep my eyes from wandering. Whenever I glanced at the faces of the other folks in church—stern-faced, harsh-seeming, joyless—I fell headlong into sin.

I wrestled with this enigma nearly every day. Why, I wondered, does the worship that brings me peace, joy, and a laughing heart appear so like a burden to these my scowling brothers and these my pucker-faced sisters?

Bottom line: they made me a little angry—a habitual sin from my past.

Then, as soon as I realized the attitude I was developing toward them, I realized that I had, in that moment, compounded my own sin, pretty much taking myself back to square one, or worse.

This, then, led to my being even more angry. Et cetera.

You get the idea. It was a long week.

My own long-standing pride didn't help one bit.

———

It was Saint Isaak of Syria who helped me break the cycle. Reading through the homilies of his "second part" in my room midweek, I was reminded—duh!—that sin is best understood as an illness. I was reminded that the Church is fairly understood as a hospital, the site of our healing. Extending that metaphor, I came to see that a monastery— especially a monastery that makes itself as available to outsiders as Saint Anthony's does—is fairly to be understood as something of a trauma center, an emergency room. This is where we can come when the ravages of our illnesses have drawn us very near to spiritual death.

I repented of my failure—a long-standing failure, actually—to love others, and the problem didn't come up again. That week, anyway.

Another took its place.

For most of this week—as I worked with the monks, savored the services, pursued prayer—I looked forward to a chance to meet and speak with Elder Ephrém. Midweek, I was cautioned by Father Arsénios—the monk who arranges these visits—that the elder is uncomfortable counseling pilgrims in English, and that because I didn't speak fluent Greek, I would more likely be visiting with Elder Paísios, the abbot. This was, actually, fine by me. My friend Seraphima had expressed great love for both men, and told me that she had been helped many times by each. As my primary hope was to discover if one of these holy men might become my spiritual guide in prayer, it made perfect sense that I should seek a father who was comfortable with English.

On Thursday, the appointed day, I arrived in the waiting area of the katholikón at 11:00 AM, just as Father Arsénios had instructed. I sat there, praying, for the next five hours, as a continuous stream of pilgrims came and went. This was a little puzzling, but I eventually realized that these others were men and women who already had long-standing relationships with the elders, whereas I was a newbie who should just be patient and wait his turn. I was flying standby.

No biggie. I sat. I prayed. I waited my turn.

A little before 4:00 PM, Father Arsénios called me to the door of the small office where Elder Paísios was hearing confessions. I entered with reverence, kissed his hand, and was immediately struck by the weariness on his face—and perhaps a subtle indifference. He was clearly worn out.

I stammered a bit about this being my first visit with an elder here in the States, and confessed that I didn't really know how to begin.

He didn't say a word.

I kept yammering, saying I had been seeking prayer for some years now, and that I didn't feel as if I were making much progress.

Not a word.

Growing more anxious, I said, "Yéronda, I'm asking for direction, for a rule of prayer. I need guidance."

He took a deep breath. He asked what my rule of prayer was, and when I'd told him, he pointed to my prayer rope and said, "Add two ropes of the Jesus Prayer and one rope to the Theotokos."

"Do you do prostrations?" he asked.

I told him that I end my prayers with the prayer of Saint Ephrém, a sequence of prayers that includes three prostrations with each repetition.

He then asked if my health was good, and when I said yes he said, "Add twenty prostrations to your evening rule, and ten to your morning rule."

I said I would.

He then went on to tell me—as my jaw dropped—about three related issues in my life that I had neither mentioned to him nor to anyone else at the monastery.

As I puzzled this stunning turn of events, he stood up.

I thought he was standing to bless me. Instead, he pointed to the door, saying, "Trápeza will start soon."

I turned to go, then turned back, standing before him and bowing. I raised my cupped hands to receive his hand, saying, "*Evlogeíte.*"

"*O Kyrios,*" he said, blessing me with the sign of the cross.

I kissed his hand, and left.

My mind was spinning.

Back in my room, I pulled my calendar from my book bag to see when I might be able to squeeze in another trip to Mount Athos. I needed to talk about these things with the fathers there.

———

The next morning, as I was passing Father Arsénios in the garden, I asked him if I might be able to meet with Elder Ephrém for just a moment; I wouldn't take up much of his time, but only hoped he might bless my prayer rope, and bless me. Father Arsénios thought this was a good idea, and told me, once again, to arrive at 11:00 AM, when he'd squeeze me in between the elder's visits with his many spiritual children.

It all sounded very likely.

I showed up at the appointed time, and—long story short—was finally called in to see the elder at about 5:00 PM, after everyone else had gone. In the meantime, I had started thinking that the Arizona elders were, at the very least, giving me a memorable lesson in patience.

Just before I was called in, Father Arsénios said that I was in luck, given that there was no one behind me—not now anyway—and I would be able to ask the elder a question or two, using Father Arsénios as my translator.

All good. *Very* good, even. Yéronda Ephrém has a reputation for being something of a clairvoyant, and my experience with Yéronda Païsios had already brought that possibility back onto my radar. Elder Ephrém is considered by many also to be one of those men whose charisma includes the ability to discern helpful solutions to difficult matters.

Inside, I bowed, kissed the elder's hand, and received his blessing. When Father Arsénios and I were seated, Father asked if I had a question for the elder. As it happened, I had a couple.

For one, I had a question about a family health matter, something that had thrown us for a bit of a loop. The yéronda replied that love, responding in love and support, was essential.

I nodded, "*Nai, nai. Efcharistó, Yéronda.*"

I also had a question having to do with a range of difficulties and concerns in our parish back home. There were a number of developments over which I had been, quite frankly, anguishing. I spoke of them as generally and as calmly as I could, asking the elder to help me understand what the best course of action would be. At least, I asked, could he help me to see how I should respond to these difficulties?

The yéronda looked at Father Arsénios with an exceedingly pained look, and said that this was a question for Elder Païsios.

I thought maybe I should rephrase the question, but I didn't have time.

Reading the situation, Father Arsénios stood up.

I followed suit. "*Evlogeíte*," I said, kissing the elder's hand. I hurried out, hoping to get to my room before anyone saw how depressed I had suddenly become. As I got to the outer door, Father Arsénios called out to me, and caught up with me on the walkway.

"I'm sorry," he said. He put his hand on my shoulder.

"It's OK, it's OK," I mumbled. "I think I squandered an opportunity here. I should have asked about prayer instead of petty parish matters. I thought maybe the yéronda might miraculously know what to say to me."

"Well, sometimes it actually happens," he said, "but it's not something you can predict, or control."

"I get that part."

"Don't be upset," he said. "Just remember his words about love; they might be the answer to both questions."

In retrospect, they were.

———

I skipped the evening trápeza, and stayed in my room praying all night. Hunger helped me focus on my prayer, kept me fairly wakeful all night. About an hour before the tálanton—about 2:00 AM—I left my room, and wandered the grounds, the gardens, praying in the cool desert air. In a very surprising way, I was feeling a mix of disappointment about my visits with the elders, disappointment in my own melancholy, and surprising delight from my exchanges with the young monks here. I was both discouraged about the prospect of finding—at Saint Anthony's—a father to guide me, and increasingly eager to return to Mount Athos to speak candidly about all of this with Father Iákovos, for one.

In short, I was feeling a little torn, but happily torn.

As I walked, I passed the katholikón and then walked along the attached building where Elders Ephrém and Paísios heard confessions and gave counsel. The lights in both men's rooms were still burning, and as I passed his window, I saw Yéronda Ephrém speaking even then to a troubled man who appeared to be sobbing. I realized that these elders' lives were not their own, that long into the night they were still giving comfort to their spiritual children.

That I wasn't to be one of them was no one's fault, unless it was my own for presuming such a relationship occurred at whim and on demand.

I kept walking.

Sitting on the lip of an unfinished fountain, and staring out into the dark of the desert, I found that the prayer proved a powerful comfort. As well as the Jesus Prayer, I was also saying certain prayers of Saint Isaak, and, in particular, I found reassuring confidence in acknowledging, "For it is You who gives prayer to those who pray."

PART THREE

THE
NEAR

14

accepted as adopted sons . . .

My son, Ben, agreed to join me on my third pilgrimage to the Holy Mountain. As the time of our departure approached, he became increasingly eager to try ascesis on for size. He said he was looking forward to the long hikes, the fasting, the physically and mentally demanding worship services. When he first signed on for this leg of the journey, I had more or less assumed I would spend another two weeks traipsing the peninsula, this time with Ben by my side; but as I studied the map and recalled the various trails and terrain, I wised up some.

My primary desire, this time out, was that I hoped Ben would love the Holy Mountain as much as I had come to love it; I wanted him to taste the stillness, and develop a hunger for it.

If he did, I knew the stillness of the Holy Mountain would become a lifelong resource for his own journey, wherever that journey took him. The last thing I wanted was for him to be *burned out* by our having taken on more than he was ready for. So, with some helpful advice in a letter from Father Iákovos and in e-mails from my friend Stelios Zarganes—one of my two Greek rescuers, and a man with whom I had continued to correspond—Ben and I planned a more reasonable route that would give us two nights at Simonópetra, two at Grigoríou, one at Saint Andrew's Skete, two nights at Vatopédi, leaving us with a final night at the lovely Xenofóndos. I was especially glad that we would be at Vatopédi for the Feast of Pentecost Sunday, including a festal vigil Saturday night. There would be plenty of hiking, but, for the most part, we would have restful days between treks, when we could stay put and pray, and experience the rhythms of Athonite life.

Stelios and his wife, Sophia, met us at the airport, and helped us get ready, giving us a restful evening of hospitality and reminiscences of Mount Athos—of Simonópetra in particular. Tryfon, their son, took a short break from his studies to spend the evening with us. He and Ben hit it off right away, and the two boys spent a good bit of the evening playing computer games and listening to music.

The family's very good friend, Father Metrophánes—the monk who'd been in charge of port operations at Dáfni, and the man who had secured speedboat passage for Stelios, Argyris, and me during the winter—had recently succumbed to cancer. He had fallen asleep. So the evening became, off and on, somewhat subdued by occasional reference to his passing, and, off and on, somewhat charged with memories of their many years together. He had been especially close to Tryfon, and one particular recollection of a snowball fight between the boy and the monk on the ridge above Simonópetra had us all in tears, if very mixed tears, both sad and joyful.

While this had been a heartbreaking experience for those around him, it had not been unexpected, and Father Metrophánes had accepted his fate with calm anticipation.

During Great Lent, the Orthodox often use the term *harmolype* (*ar mo LEE peh*)—sometimes translated as "bright sadness"—in an attempt to articulate the curious emotion that infuses the Lenten fasting period before the Feast of Pascha. The two-sided coin of that term serves to reveal this curious mix of both grief and promise that—I gathered from what the family was saying—also infused Father Metrophánes's last days among his brothers at Simonópetra.

Stelios went to a cabinet in the living room, and lifted a *komvoskíni*—a prayer rope—from where it had been hanging on a knob. He brought it to me, and laid it in my hands. "Father Metrophánes's prayer rope," he said. "Now it's mine. I want to take very good care of it."

———

In the morning, Stelios fetched Ben and me from our hotel and—after lavishly feeding us again and loading us up with a sack of Sophia's homemade *tirópita* (cheese pies) to sustain us for the short term—he dropped us at the KTEL, where we boarded the bus for Ouranoúpoli.

I again enjoyed the tour of the countryside, but mostly enjoyed watching Ben's response to the landscape and villages; he studied every nook and cranny and *ouzería* along the way, and by the time our three-hour bus ride ended, he was already talking with confidence about the year he would be living in Greece between high school and college. To myself, I was thinking, *Maybe after college.*

Ouranoúpoli itself was Ben's idea of the perfect town—small, coastal, full of friendly people and great food.

Much as Nick and I had done in September, Ben and I savored our first evening in Ouranoúpoli at a seaside café—the same café, actually—taking in the sights, sounds, smells, and tastes, gazing as far as we could down the peninsula to where the Holy Mountain disappeared into a darkening purple sky.

———

Morning found us up before dawn, packing our gear into backpacks, then scrambling to gather our diamonitíria, our boat tickets, and a quick breakfast before boarding the *Áxion Estín* and setting off onto an impossibly blue Aegean Sea. The boat was, again, filled to overflowing with monks, workmen, and a wide array of pilgrims. There seemed to be less beer.

"We're on our way now," Ben said, giving about as wide a grin as I've ever seen, his silver braces sparkling.

On board, we met half a dozen men from America, including a priest and a deacon, who were part of an Orthodox tour group arranged by Saint Herman's Seminary in Alaska. I was also pleased to see, yet again, the Bulgarian monk I'd first seen in September at the Thessaloníki bus station, the KTEL, scratching at a lottery ticket. I'd seen him a second time in December praying on the boat, and here he was yet again, leaning against the stern rail, looking off into the distance, prayer rope in hand.

When we reached Dáfni, Ben and I scrambled through the crowd to the port's back forty, where—as directed by Stelios—we would meet the microbus to Simonópetra.

—— *Coming Home to Simonópetra* ——

Father Iákovos was waiting for us when we arrived, as was the novice Níkos, who was still here, with a somewhat fuller beard. We were greeted with humbling warmth. Once again, as he embraced me, Father Iákovos said, "Welcome home."

The way they all responded to Ben—rather, *Venyamín*—was an added perk. He was immediately taken underwing as a favorite grandson. Within minutes, he'd met a good dozen monks, young and old, and they loaded him up with loukoúmi and hard candies to stick in his pocket for later.

In particular, we met Father Andrew, the gregarious guestmaster, who, we learned, was the son of another of the fathers there at Simonópetra. Their story is an amazing one, a genuinely humbling one. I had met Father George, the father of the pair, during the first day of my visit in the wintertime. He had struck me immediately with a glowing warmth, a ready kindness. Corny as it will no doubt sound, one of my most treasured moments of that pilgrimage was in the midst of washing dishes with Níkos on my second day at Simonópetra, when Father George happened by, watched us a moment, then said, "Isaák, Isaák," his face positively beaming. It seems like such a slight gesture, perhaps, but literally—and yes, I do mean *literally*—it had warmed my heart.

Now I was learning from Father Iákovos that the monk I was meeting now—this storytelling Father Andrew—was Father George's son. The father, it turns out, had followed the son into monasticism. More surprising yet, Father George's daughter serves as the yeróndessa, the abbess, of the convent at Ormylia, where—*get this*—both another sister and their mother also serve as nuns. The youngest daughter of the family is the *presvytéra*, the wife, of another Father Andrew, the priest who serves in Thessaloníki at Simonópetra's *Metóchion*, which is something like an embassy church representing the monastery in the local diocese. While we visited in the archondaríki with Father Iákovos, Father Andrew, and Níkos, Father George stopped by as well. He was exceedingly happy to play grandfather to Ben, dropping a handful of hard candies into his hands. By the time Vespers came around, Ben knew his way around the place as if he'd been there many times before.

———

Vespers at Simonópetra is, of course, always beautiful, always moving, but this time, as I inhaled the censed air of the katholikón, savored the beauty of the icons, intoned the Vespers hymns under my breath, and prayed the prayers, it was all the more sweet to look over from time to time to see my son in the stall next to me, his eyes wide with interest, his smile intermittently brightening, at least for me, our already luminous evening prayer.

Following trápeza, we venerated the relics in the katholikón, and, in particular, Ben was able to feel for himself the warmth of Saint Mary Magdalene's hand on his lips. "Hey," he said, "you weren't kidding."

Father Theológos—the priest charged with the care of the relics—blessed our prayer ropes with the relics, and we headed out to meet Father Iákovos and Níkos in the archondaríki, where Níkos was "on duty." After another round of loukoúmi and coffee, Ben and I strolled down the slope with Father Iákovos to his dental office, where he brewed his customary pot of mountain tea. We sat on the balcony outside—at the very brink of the rock face—savoring the cool evening, the hot tea, the astonishing view of the sea. A good number of bats added an impressive air show in the expanse before us.

We talked about a good many things, mostly about cultivating a life of prayer. Father Iákovos shared some insights he'd gained from his Yéronda Aimilianós; in particular, he said to Ben, "Just as our lungs breathe air, so our souls breathe prayer. Our souls cannot develop, cannot survive without prayer."

I was content to sit quietly, attending to Ben's receiving instruction from Father Iákovos; I was also breathing the prayer in silence.

Late in the evening, Father Iákovos asked Ben what he planned to be when he grew up. Ben's answer surprised even me. "I was thinking I might want to become a priest."

I hadn't heard about any such thinking.

Father Iákovos asked, "What about being a monk?"

My son Ben is probably the most good-hearted, most sensitive to other people's feelings of any kid you're likely to meet, so I know it was hard for him to say what he said next. "I *would* be a monk . . . except that I want to have a wife and kids. I like my family; I want to have one just like it."

"Ah," said Father Iákovos, "those are good plans. You probably shouldn't be a monk then." He was smiling broadly as he refilled our cups.

As Ben and I walked back up the cobbles to the guesthouse, he stopped midway in the path, turned to look out at the amazing night sky over the sea, breathed a big sigh, and said, with a skateboarder's inflection, "Whoa, this is *sweet!*"

———

If I had been concerned that Ben would be slow to rise for the midnight services, that concern vanished when *he* was the one who woke *me* at 3:00 AM, a good five minutes before the tálanton sounded. You have to know a bit about our "normal" lives to appreciate this phenomenon. Like most fourteen-year-olds, Ben pretty much has to be dragged out of bed most mornings. On the weekends, he can easily sleep until noon or later, regardless of when he goes to bed the night before.

He was dressed and ready before I was, and we climbed up the causeway to the katholikón well before any other pilgrims, and ahead of many monks.

I had been anxious, as well, that Ben wouldn't be able to stay alert, or even awake, through the nearly four hours of worship—but I shouldn't have worried. His eyes were bright with interest from the first prayers to the last.

In the midst of orthros, Father Michael, the priest who was serving at the altar during our stay, stepped over to us and asked if he could borrow Ben for a moment. They disappeared for about ten minutes, returning just before Father Michael needed to return to the altar.

"What's up?" I whispered to Ben.

"He showed me where I'll be working after breakfast." Ben was clearly pleased to be included in the work at hand. "I get to help bake the bread."

———

After we'd received Communion—Ben just ahead of me in line—I could hardly see my way back to my stall, having been completely undone by the sight of Ben's receiving the Holy Mysteries on the Holy Mountain.

It is a wonderful thing to pursue the prayer of the heart, a wonderful thing to proceed along the way of a pilgrim. It is far better to proceed along that way with another.

This understanding would continue to enrich this third pilgrimage with a more poignant sense of joy, but at this moment—standing in the stall beside my son as the liturgy concluded in "We have seen the

Light, the True Light, and have received the Heavenly Spirit . . ."—I was convinced once and for all that the heart of the matter was our finding our way together.

———

As I must have suggested by now, over the years since my leaving home for college, salvation itself has come to mean something larger to me, fuller, more substantial and more immediate than, say, the commonplace version of a personal, late-hour reprieve from execution, or my dodging a stint in Gehenna. For the Orthodox, salvation, or "being saved," indicates a process, rather than a moment. It is a process of being redeemed from separation from God, both *now* and ever. It has very little to do with the popular notion of "going to heaven." Moreover, the Orthodox have insisted, from their earliest canons on the matter, that salvation belongs to all humankind, not just to members of the Orthodox Church. Of course, they also insist that the most trustworthy road to participation in the saving life of God is revealed in the traditional teaching of that very Church.

For me, in any case, salvation has come to mean deliverance, and now, from the death-in-life routine that we often settle for—the somnambulate life for which *I* have often settled. Somehow related to this is another, developing sense that while salvation happens to persons, it is not a simply personal manner.

I like very much the response that Father Iákovos gave to a man who interrupted our conversation to ask the monk if Jesus Christ was his "personal savior."

"Nope," he said, "I like to share him."

Thanks to Father Iákovos and the tradition he manifests, I have a developing sense that salvation must have to do with all of us, collectively, and that it must have to do with all else as well—all of creation, in fact.

It turns out that I am not alone in my thinking so.

My reading in the Fathers and the Mothers of the Church—as well as my late return to what I would call *midrashic* Bible-reading—has me thinking that all creation is implicated in this phenomenon we call salvation, redemption, reconciliation. Like the late theologian John Romanides, I've come to suspect that our saving relationship with God is "as the Body of Christ," not a discrete, individualized, private relationship, but a *member*ship in a Body that is at once both alive and life-giving.

I have a good number of beloved friends, men and women who, if you were to meet them, you would recognize immediately as genuinely spiritual people, but some of whom have yet to find a body to which to belong. They are, as I say, beautiful, kind, deeply spiritual believers of one stripe or another; they also share, paradoxically, a compelling hunger for community, which they intentionally pursue in a number of worthwhile activities—community choirs, potluck dinners, block parties, arts conferences. They also—it so happens—share an abiding sense of alienation from the Body of Christ, as that Body is expressed in the media and, tragically, in their local churches. Each has also, I daresay, survived a number of clumsy, insensitive, and frankly idiotic ordeals in one or more of those communities.

Be that as it may, I think that—somehow or other and regardless— they *must* find a way home, a way to reconnect their faith to their communities and their communities to their faith—a way to reconnect, as it were, the spirit to the body. I've been relatively late in coming to this myself, but I see now how we are called to work out this business together, and I see that faith is not something that can be both solitary and healthy. The health and fruitfulness of the severed limb depends— utterly—upon its being grafted onto the living tree.

This is what I suspect Dietrich Bonhoeffer is reintroducing to his community when he observes in *Life Together* (a book in which he wrestles to reclaim *some* of the treasure jettisoned by the Reformation, most specifically the sacrament of confession) that "the Christ in one's own heart is weaker than the Christ in the heart of one's brother." He insists that the presence of the brother—or, rather, the presence of Christ as borne by that brother—shores up one's own faith. This is, in part, also why among the ruling monasteries of Mount Athos the aberrant, idiorrythmic rule has been set aside in favor of the more deeply traditional coenobitic rule.

Dwelling somewhere at the heart of this business lies the Orthodox understanding of the human person, an understanding that commences with the conviction that we—every one of us, of whatever religion or nonreligion—are made in the image of God, and that we continue to *bear* His image, regardless of whether we do it well or badly. As the Orthodox like to say, we are written as the *icon* of God. What may come as news to some, even so, is that the *one* God is said to exist in *three* Persons engaged in a single *perichorésis*—a single circling dance—and that our trope of *Trinity*, then, is one way of figuring God Himself as an *essentially* relational being.

The Image-bearing human person—it follows—is also, necessarily, a relational being, so much so that for the Orthodox an individual is not the same thing as a person; genuine personhood stipulates the communion of one with another.

Simply put, an isolated individual does not a person make.

———

Similarly, I have a developing sense that salvation is not to be understood merely as a *future* condition, but as a moment-by-moment, *present* mode of being; I have begun to think that this is what Jesus teaches when he said, "The kingdom of heaven is within you."

I also think this is what he may have been teaching us when he announced, "Assuredly, I say to you that there are some standing here who will not taste death till they see the kingdom of God present with power." This is yet another passage we chose not to scrutinize at the Baptist church of my youth, probably because, in what I would call our narrowly apocalyptic sense of the kingdom of God, we wondered if Jesus had misspoken. Jesus, as it turns out, did not misspeak; there were, without question, among his exponentially expanding band of followers, "some standing . . . who would not taste death" before they had witnessed the kingdom, tasted its power, savored its abundant life.

According to the Fathers, this is a kingdom, a power, and a life that is no less apprehensible now.

Abba Benjamin of Scetis, one of the more obscure and most ascetic of the Desert Fathers, is said to have left his spiritual children—as he lay dying—with the following paraphrase of Saint Paul's message to the Thessalonians: "If you observe the following, you can be saved, 'Be joyful at all times, pray without ceasing, and give thanks for all things.'" Here again, I hear the words of one who is speaking from within the kingdom already. The one who apprehends the reality of God's unfailing presence, the one who sustains ongoing conversation with that Holy Presence, is able to apprehend *all things* and all experiences—the good, the bad, the beautiful, the ugly—as purposeful. That blessed person is able, even through his or her tears, to taste and to see that the Lord is good.

And so, in other words, I want very much to be saved from what passes for myself. This is because what passes for myself does not, always, feel quite like the self framed in the image of God and thus united with those around me—allegedly growing with them into His likeness.

I'd like to replace this perennially hamstrung, broken self with the more promising image. I'd like to undergo some lasting re-*pairing* of heart and mind, body and soul. And I see that it's not something one does alone.

———

Following Ben's shift in the bakery—he was in charge of loading the loaves into the stone oven, and pulling them out with the paddle—we met in the archondaríki, where, much to my surprise, Ben lifted a shot of rakí from the tray and downed it. His eyes watered a bit, but he said, "Mmmm. That's good." He followed it with a cup of Greek coffee. "That's good, too," he said. "All good."

We then hiked along the ridge behind the monastery a bit, and visited the cave of Saint Simon—where the founder of the monastery had lived before the miraculous visions that led to his founding the brotherhood here. We also descended into the heart of the monastery itself, descending a series of stairways to the library, where the bare granite of "Simon's Rock" serves as a wall in a good many of the interior rooms.

Father Michael was in the midst of his translation work, but took a break to give us a personal tour of the many ancient texts the library holds—manuscripts of patristic writers, hand-written copies of the Greek philosophers, the earliest printed editions of *The Philokalía* and *The Ladder of Divine Ascent*, works of Evagrios and Saint Gregory Palamás, and many other treasures.

———

In the evening, following trápeza, we met again with Father Iákovos. This time, we were joined by several other pilgrims, including our roommate, yet another Nick, this time from Chicago, a friendly, pious man whose wife was the niece of the beloved Yéronda Aimilianós.

We sat together on a low stone wall outside the monastery gate, the opening to the causeway that leads to the katholikón. Father Iákovos shared with us the story of his becoming a monk, how his decision had, at first, broken his father's heart. "He told me that I had taken ten years off his life."

It wasn't until some years had passed, when his father finally came to visit him at Simonópetra, that the two were able to fully reconcile. "He came to the Holy Mountain, experienced the beauty here, saw how happy I was, and he said to me, 'I told you once that you'd taken ten years off my life. Well, you've given them back. Ten years and more.'"

Father Iákovos continued speaking about the monk's relationship with his parents. "It's natural for a parent not to want this, his child going off to a monastery, no? When someone becomes a monk, he dies to the world. His eyes are on God alone. The monk is alive *in* the world, but he is dead *to* the world."

He sat for a moment, looking up at the ridge above the monastery. We could still make out the location of Saint Simon's cave. "What parent," he asked, "would be happy at the death of his child? This is why they weep when we come here. Still," he brightened, "as I told my mother once, 'Every tear you shed for the loss of your son will become as a diamond in your crown.'"

Ben and I looked at one another, saying nothing.

"While I was still a novice," Father Iákovos said, smiling, "Yéronda Aimilianós called me to his office. I walked in, received his blessing, and sat down. As I sat, I sighed. I didn't mean to! It just came out on its own. He heard that sigh, and immediately said, 'Come on. Let it out. What's troubling you?'"

Father Iákovos was very quiet for a moment, and I supposed he was feeling again the emotions of that conversation. "I looked at him and asked, 'Will my parents ever be at peace with my being here? Will they ever know how happy I am?'

"The yéronda leaned forward to meet my eyes directly, and he said, 'If you're genuinely happy, full of joy, they *will* know it. The man of prayer,' he said, 'is very like a woman who is pregnant; as she feeds herself, she also nourishes her child. The one who prays is attached, by a spiritual cord, to everyone he ever met. As he feeds himself spiritually, he also nourishes everyone else through his prayers. This is why the monk repeats, over and over again, the Jesus Prayer—he knows that as he prays for himself, he prays for everyone else. His prayer is universal.'"

Father Iákovos was beaming now. "That was all I needed to hear."

———

This was also when I learned that Father Iákovos was not yet a priest, because he then told us that in just a few weeks, on July 13— less than a month after our visit—he would be ordained into the holy priesthood, and his father would be arriving for the event.

I realized that time was running out for us; Ben and I would be leaving after trápeza in the morning. So I jumped in with some thoughts that had been gnawing at me. I told Father Iákovos that I had gone to Saint Anthony's Monastery in Arizona, hoping to find, as he had suggested, a father closer to home.

And I admitted how conflicted I'd felt during my visit there, torn between being drawn by the joy manifested by the monks and being somewhat repelled by the severity, the apparent joylessness, of many who worshiped there, using the monastery's katholikón as their parish church.

I was conscious of not wanting to speak too candidly, too critically, in front of Ben about how some expressions of Orthodoxy in general, and of monasticism in particular, struck me as more efficacious than others; still, if I was mistaken, I wanted very much to be corrected. I trusted Father Iákovos to correct me if he saw fit.

He sat back, and listened silently. Then he expressed concern about a monastery church becoming a parish for people who might live nearby, but he also spoke about the great blessing it is for those same people to have a monastery close to home. "It is a phenomenon occurring throughout history, " he said. "People have always come to the desert to see an ascetic or visit a monastery. And they often build dwellings around the cave of a hermit! Just as the hymn announces— 'The desert has blossomed as a lily, O Lord!'"

He agreed with me, even so, that there was, and still is, a range of diverse expressions of monastic life. My own thoughts were that some appeared a good deal more compelling than others.

"My sense is," I told him, "that even on Mount Athos, there appears to be something of a spectrum. On one end of that spectrum, you find Simonópetra and, perhaps, Vatopédi—open, embracing, full of joy; on the other end, one finds, say, Philothéou or Great Lavra—careful, suspicious-seeming, severe."

Father Iákovos was firmly unwilling to characterize the other monasteries, but said, "All the monasteries on the Holy Mountain make up the garden of the Panagía. As in any garden, you'll find many different flowers. Each has its own beauty, its own character, its own scent."

He laughed. "I love the sweetness of the rose. You may love the pungent scent of the gardenia. On the Holy Mountain, every man can find a monastery that speaks to his own soul."

The rub, as I saw it, was that of that wide spectrum, that surprising variety of expressions of genuine religious life, America had so far received just one end.

I didn't say much more about it, but already my imagination was spinning out a very attractive, if exceedingly speculative, future:

What if Father Iákovos himself were to be sent back to America to help found a monastery, a monastery in the spirit of Simonópetra—open, embracing, and full of joy? What if he could *then* become my spiritual father? And Benjamin's? And father to my wife Marcia and our daughter Elizabeth!

May it be blessed!

———

We turned in soon thereafter. Ben and I said our prayers, did our prostrations, and hopped into our beds. The tálanton rang out, it seemed, in no time at all.

Once again, Ben seemed already adapted to the odd hours; he was alert and active throughout the long services, even poking me in the ribs whenever he thought I was singing too loudly.

We partook of the Holy Mysteries, and then broke our fast with the fathers at trápeza. In the courtyard afterward, all the monks who had befriended us gathered around to say their good-byes—Father Iákovos, Father Michael, Father Andrew, Father George, as well as Fathers Iosíf, Pávlo, and others who had made my earlier visits to Simonópetra so rich and welcoming. Níkos was there, too, wishing us a good journey, and also helping to translate the farewells between us and the fathers.

My previous partings from this place had been softened by my knowing I'd be back soon. This time, the ache of parting was a bit more acute, as I wasn't sure exactly when I'd be back again.

Fathers George and Andrew—father and son—stood before Ben and me, pointing to themselves and to us, asking, according to Níkos, "Do you see the resemblance?"

In turn, each monk kissed us good-bye, embraced us with great warmth. Ben was beaming, but speechless; I could see how moved he was, and that further thickened the lump in my throat.

Father Andrew stood before me a final time, taking my hand and saying we would meet again. I said to him, "You must bring Simonópetra to America. *Please*."

He laughed and said, "Just find us the right rock."

15

What I say to you, I say to all—Watch!

B en was pretty quiet for most of the hour it took us to hike down the slope to Grigoríou. At the top of the headland, however, he turned to me and asked, "Can we come back here sometime?"

"Probably not on this trip," I answered.

"Oh, I know. I didn't mean *this* trip; I just want to know that we get to come back sometime. I love it here."

"That's not just the rakí talking, is it?"

"No, I don't think so."

"Yep. I love it, too. Let's be sure to come back."

At the bottom of the slope, the trail passed along a pebbled beach. We dropped our packs on the rocks and took a rest there, wading in the warm water, inhaling the salt air, and skipping rocks. Ben reached into his pack and pulled out a full box of loukoúmi.

"Where'd you get that?" I asked him.

"Father Andrew," he said, popping a square into his mouth. His smiling lips were covered in powdered sugar; so was his chin. "It's the good kind, green, lots of nuts."

We arrived at the arsanás of Grigoríou just ahead of the *Ágia Ánna*, which was, by the look of it, loaded with quite a pile o' pilgrims. Ben and I picked up the pace, so we could arrive at the upper archondaríki in time to say hello to Father Cosmás before the crowd arrived.

We found him in the archondaríki kitchen, boiling coffee for the coming onslaught. When he saw us, he put it aside, howling, "Isaák! It's about time you showed up!" He pointed to Ben, "Who's this? Your father?"

———

He hurried us into seats at the table in the kitchen, telling us to make ourselves at home while he got the coffee served to the others.

During our two days at Grigoríou, we spent a good bit of time at that kitchen table, visiting with Father Cosmás, and with our second roommate—also named Nick—who was making his annual visit to Mount Athos to see his spiritual father, a yéronda he shared with Father Cosmás. The two of them were, therefore, as they put it, brothers.

Along the way, Ben was able to visit the cemetery chapel and the very full ossuary. Later, he said to me, "That was really something, the bones of all those monks."

"Did you think it was strange?" I asked him.

"Sure. It *is* strange. But not in a bad way."

Ben also liked that "they recycle the graves," removing the bones from the ground, and "making room for the next guy."

––––––

My time with Father Cosmás was, all told, too brief; but he did take the chance to ask me how my journey to prayer was faring. I told him that it was still a matter of ups and downs. The ups were, perhaps, increasing in duration, but the downs remained a constant threat.

"They will always be a constant threat," he said. "Stillness," he said, "is a worthy aim, and watchfulness—*népsis*—is its strongest protection. You must guard your heart against a lot, of course, but mostly against the illusion that you can ever let down your guard, even for a minute.

"The enemy's greatest threat is letting us think he is no longer a threat."

What he said pretty much reminded me of me. Most times—make that every time—I've gone through what I would call a detour from prayer and a subsequent eruption of anger and/or pride, that descent was preceded by my thinking I might just skip a prayer or two, take a little break, given how well things were going.

Even a little *break*, it seems, can leave you *broken*—and wondering how you got that way.

My own greatest sin—I was thinking just then—pretty much boils down to pride, and to the countless attendant sins that pride makes possible.

"Watchfulness," Father Cosmás was saying, "also involves seeing your sin and your own sinfulness. If you see your own sin, you will be spared the most insidious sin, the greatest sin, which is pride."

Ouch.

Yep—I told him—that pretty much hits me where I live.

"Me, too," he said. "How do you think I learned any of this?"

———

Our next stop was Saint Andrew's Skete near Karyés. We would need to renew our diamonitíria before heading on to Vatopédi, so planned to stay one night at the skete. My last time here—during the Feast of Saint Andrew—the place had been packed with hundreds of guests. This time, Ben and I were two among perhaps thirty or so.

Once we'd been led to our room, a very cozy room with two beds, and—in welcomed contrast to the room I'd had in the winter here—window glass in the window frame, Ben and I hiked into Karyés, thinking we might get our permits extended and have done with it. The Pilgrims' Bureau offices were closed, so we'd have to make another try in the morning. Meantime, we had a chance to walk around the village, poking around the icon shops, and picking up a pile of prayer ropes and other gifts to take back home.

———

Back at the skete, we took what we thought would be a shortcut back to the archondaríki. It turned out to be not so short, but it did offer a surprising glimpse of how extensive the ruins of the skete were. I had already guessed that only a very small percentage of the skete had been restored, but we spent most of an hour wandering through a maze of burned-out buildings, some of which had become full of trees and grasses, and a good many of which were all but erased from view by the crumbling destruction of their walls amid the flourishing overgrowth.

When we'd found our way back to the main courtyard again, we passed by a youngish, roundish monk, with his foot propped up on the wall he sat upon. "*Evlogeíte*," I said.

"*O Kyrios,*" he responded. Then he said, in English, "Where are you from?"

This turned out to be yet another Father Ephrém, an English monk whom Father Cosmás had suggested we try to meet. Limping slightly— he'd broken his ankle earlier in the year—he led us into the famously enormous kyriakón, and to the chapel area to the left of the central nave, where Vespers was about to begin.

The chanting was erratic, and not entirely pleasing. I had a very strong sense that the monks doing the chanting were doing so under duress. In fact, when Father Ephrém was directed, at one unconsidered point, to intone a short sequence of hymns, the pain on his face made it clear that he knew he could not carry a note. He was not the only one.

When it was over, I was exhausted. Ben had pretty much kept his own counsel, but as Father Ephrém led us to trápeza, Ben said to him, "That was nice."

"You shouldn't lie, Benjamin," was Father Ephrém's smiling response.

———

We made plans to meet with Father Ephrém after trápeza in the morning. He had offered to give us an insider's tour of the katholikón. Then Ben and I turned in for the night. The sparse food, the long hours, and the relatively little sleep we'd had—four days running—were beginning to take a toll on us both, especially on Ben, who'd hadn't run this particular gauntlet before, nor anything vaguely approaching it. We lay down on our beds, and when, within seconds, I asked Ben if he wanted some water, he didn't answer. He was already asleep.

———

The tálanton just barely managed to rouse me, and looking across the room I saw that Ben hadn't heard it at all. I mulled over the right thing to do, and decided I would let him sleep through the midnight service, and wake him in time for orthros. I turned on my flashlight to read, opening to Yéronda Aimilianós's "Catechism on Prayer."

I remember some of what I read, but what I remember far more vividly is waking up again with a start, my flashlight in hand, my head jerking up from where it had fallen into the open book.

I looked at my watch, and realized that we were probably missing orthros.

Ben woke up pretty quickly at that point, and I was suddenly alert as well. We dressed in a rush, and more or less jogged across the courtyard to the katholikón, venerated the icons in the narthex, then entered the nave in time to hear the priest intone, *Evlogiméni i Vasileía tou Patrós kai tou Yióu kai tou Ágiou Pnévmatos*—the opening words of the Divine Liturgy.

Ben and I made our way down the hundred or so yards of echoing nave to two empty stalls near the front. As the litany continued, we went forward to venerate the icons. A few other men joined us, and I was a little relieved that we were not the only latecomers.

After liturgy, we received antídoron, then had time to venerate the many icons on our way out. By the time we'd gotten outside, there wasn't another soul in sight; we walked around to the side of the building and to the entry to the trápeza, only to find that it was chained shut. We supposed that the skete might observe a rest time between liturgy and trápeza, as often happens, say, at Simonópetra and Grigoríou, so we thought we should take the chance to rest. The microbus to Vatopédi wouldn't be leaving until after 2:00 PM.

After half an hour or so, I left Ben napping in the room, and hiked in to Karyés to get our diamonitíria extended. The official did so with no problem, pleasantly even, and I hurried back to the skete. In the courtyard, there was still no sign of life around the chained trápeza door, so I joined Ben in the room and lay down for further rest, thinking the bell for breakfast would rouse us eventually.

I was awakened at noon by a knocking at the door; it was the guestmaster asking if we wanted to stay another night. No, I told him, we thought we'd head into town after trápeza to catch the bus to Vatopédi.

"Trápeza?" he said. "Trápeza is over hours ago."

Evidently, while Ben and I were venerating icons after liturgy, the community had made its way to yet another dining area, a smaller trápeza that I didn't know anything about. The guestmaster was chagrined, and insisted that we let him make us a tray in the archondaríki. He loaded us up with apples, biscotti, and loukoúmi; he made coffee, and he insisted we finish up with big, sticky squares of baklava. We cooperated as well as we could, then thanked him and donned our packs for the hike into town.

My experiences throughout the Holy Mountain have been, almost completely, wonderful; even when I wasn't especially pleased with, say, a particular monastery's attitude toward—or treatment of—pilgrims, I realized they surely had their reasons. That said, there are two places on the peninsula where I more or less came to expect to lose a bit of spiritual ground—Dáfni, the port of entry, and Karyés, the center of government. These happen to be the only places where pilgrims tend to outnumber—and by a significant margin—the monks. These are also the only places where large groups of nonmonastic Athonites pretty much call the shots, especially in terms of transportation.

To be fair, these men may also have good reason for the general callousness they display. Pilgrims can be painfully misinformed; they can be oblivious to local conventions and even the most elementary religious practices. Pilgrims can manifest a profound and aggravating sense of entitlement. Pilgrims, in short, can be jerks. The odds, therefore, are pretty good that the men who drive the microbuses, day in and day out, have good cause to manifest—as many do—a disposition of *not giving a damn*, if only as a form of self-preservation. Beyond that, the weekends of major feasts—like Pentecost, for instance—load the logistical infrastructure to its breaking point. Whatever.

In any case, the only times I've nearly blown my stack on Mount Athos had to do with trying to get from one place to another using the transportation these guys are allegedly there to supply. When I was traveling alone—that is, when it was only a matter of *my* getting where I needed to go—the frustrations were somehow more tolerable, even sometimes comically entertaining; when, however, these gentlemen extended their crap to my son, and when, for instance, one of the drivers roughly pushed Ben out of the way as he hopped into his microbus, I thought for a minute that I might reach up through his open window, grab him by the throat, and drag him out for a lesson in manners. As it was, I called him in Greek the worst thing I could think of to call him. Whatever stillness, calm, and prayerful humility I had discovered at the monasteries were pretty much squandered here in Karyés. I had suddenly lost a lot of ground.

I'm not entirely alone in this. Ben and I met a wonderful pilgrim from the States, a publisher named Art Dimopoulos who, we learned, regularly spends time at Koutloumousíou. When we'd all finally made it onto a bus out of Karyés, he said to me: "It never fails. You can spend three days in the monastery, discover a very deep sense of peace, and it's all gone in fifteen minutes trying to get on the bus."

I don't know.

Take it as a warning.

Well warned is well armed.

Maybe.

At any rate, Ben and I may have been the first ones to arrive for the microbus to Vatopédi, but we didn't manage actually to get on it. We suffered a series of misdirections that led to large crowds of men pushing and shoving from one bus to the next, angrily demanding to know which bus was going where, and led to our being given bad information again and again. Ben and I decided, finally, to sit it out and see what would come. We watched as the pilgrim-mob turned pretty ugly, then scrapped and screamed to get their desired seats.

When the dust had cleared, Ben and I were all but alone, sitting on the curb, asking whoever passed by if they knew a way to Vatopédi. Two men from Sófia sidled up next to us and let us know that they were going that direction, too, not all the way to Vatopédi, but to a skete along the way. We four sat, then, waiting for something good to happen.

Then it did.

A monk stopped by to tell us he had found us a ride. The ride he'd found was a Datsun pickup truck driven by a weathered old guy named Ioánis.

Ioánis—I was soon to learn—made his living by charging exorbitant fees for rides late in the day; he more or less counted on folks like us to be desperate enough to pay. Initially, he agreed to a cool seventy euros to haul all four of us down the road; by the time it was over, he'd gotten seventy euros from Ben and me, and another seventy euros from the two Bulgarians. The drive took about forty minutes.

When we got to the first checkpoint—the first gate protecting Vatopédi from unexpected guests—the officer checked to see if our names were on the list to be let through. When we said we were Isaák and Venyamín, he lit up, saying, *Ne, ne, Pater Matteou! Pater Matteou!* Evidently, Father Matthew, who'd gotten us on the list in the first place, was a favorite with this gatekeeper. This particular officer—who must also have had something of a history with our driver—put his finger about an inch from Ioánis's nose, and, I'm pretty sure, asked him how far he was taking us. From what I gathered, Ioánis had planned on leaving us with the Bulgarians at their destination, dropping us about two miles short of Vatopédi.

At that point, it sounded—in very fast and very loud Greek of an undeniably urban sort—as if the gatekeeper were, you might say, tearing Ioánis a new one, and thereby got the suddenly accommodating driver to promise to take us to the Vatopédi gate. He made Ioánis say as much. He made him say it three times.

Along the way, we dropped the Bulgarians at *their* destination, *Skíti Vogorodítsa*—the Skete of the Dormition of the Theotokos—one of the very earliest Bulgarian sketes on the Holy Mountain, and one that looks, from the outside, a little like a walled-up junkyard in the middle of thick chestnut forest. Once the monks unbar the huge, if rickety, wooden gate from the inside, however, a well-maintained, very-close-quartered garden of paradise is revealed within. We stopped long enough to venerate the very old icons inside the katholikón, which is dedicated to the Assumption of the Theotokos; we also received the blessing of the Bulgarian priest-monk who'd let us in. All in all, it was a quite a beautiful surprise.

As Ben and I squeezed back inside the Datsun truck, even Ioánis seemed more likeable. He drove us the rest of the way to Vatopédi, even deigning to converse a bit in English, which, it turned out, he could do fairly well. His good-bye included a final dose of "I like Americans. I no like America."

We arrived at the gate around 4:30, well after the other visitors; Vespers had already begun, but we were welcomed readily by the gatekeeper, and directed to the archondaríki. Again, as we were being checked in, the guestmaster took care to make our reservations for the bus two days hence and, while he was at it, asked if we would like to go to confession while we were here.

My new rule: whenever anyone asks if I want to go to confession, I will say yes.

I said yes. And, surprisingly—to me at least—so did Ben. We would be called out from the all-night vigil to see Father Gregory, the same priest with whom I had made my confession during the winter.

We had just enough time to drop our bags in the room and throw water on our faces before heading to trápeza, where we came in at the end of an amazing crowd of pilgrims. Pentecost had filled the guest rooms to capacity, and very nearly filled the enormous trápeza as well. I realized afresh how generous Father Matthew had been to arrange two nights for us at such a busy time.

Speaking of Father Matthew, he found us in the courtyard after trápeza, and after warmly embracing us both, led us into the katholikón to venerate the relics, where he once more supplied an English translation of the priest's words. Here again, just as during my winter visit, I was especially and oddly moved by the belt of the Theotokos. An inexplicable sweetness and powerful sense of presence accompanied my kissing this strip of ancient fabric that had, as I imagined it, wound around the very womb that one time proved to be, as we like to say, "more spacious than the heavens"—containing, as it did, the uncontainable God.

Afterward, Father Matthew led us to venerate the several miracle-working icons throughout the katholikón and in the adjoining chapels, giving Ben the full stories of each, including Our Lady *Paramythía*, an icon that had spoken aloud to warn the gatekeepers about pirates lurking outside, Our Lady *Esphagméni*, an icon that had been attacked by a prideful monk, and Our Lady *Pantánassa*, an icon that continues to this day to bring healing to thousands with cancer, especially many hundreds of children afflicted in the Ukraine following the disaster at Chernobyl.

As Father Matthew excused himself to prepare for the vigil, he suggested we might want to rest a bit before coming back. We probably should have taken his advice; as it was, Ben and I strolled around the grounds, getting a better sense of the significant spread of the monastery—a mix of ancient dwellings and new construction, a broad collection of cottage industry and agriculture, and all of it apparently thriving.

The familiar tálanton called us back inside.

Once again, we were able to find chairs in the katholikón's central nave just as the vigil began, but Ben soon suggested we snag a couple stalls that had opened up behind us. We had both come to appreciate the way the old-style stalls could facilitate sitting, standing, and leaning, allowing us to remain in place for hours without, say, having our butts fall asleep.

A couple hours into the vigil, the guestmaster drew us out to wait in stalls outside the chapel of Saint Dimítrios to the left of the narthex. We waited there for a good while, listening to the Vesper hymns, staring into the icon of the Theotokos, Our Lady Esphagméni—Our Lady *Slain*—which commanded the dark wall before us. Long ago, a monk in a fit of pride and rage had driven a knife into the cheek of this icon. It had bled. That same monk spent the rest of his life in anguished repentance, sitting precisely where we were sitting now. The overall situation was, I'd say, a good inducement to our preparing for confession.

As Ben was called in, I prayed that he might be both strong and brave enough to speak without fear. I finished by praying the same for myself.

When my turn came, I found Father Gregory pretty much in the same spot I'd met him six months earlier. I'm sure he didn't remember me, but I reminded him that he had helped me once before. Then, I confessed my usual—fairly habitual—sins of pride and an appalling lack of love for people in general. Father Gregory suggested I regularly include the prayer of Saint Ephrém in my rule, and I told him that I already did.

He looked at me a minute, then said, "You have to mean it."

Alrightythen.

I moved on to what was most on my mind. "Father," I said, "I have been saying the Jesus Prayer for close to ten years, without finding my way to a life of prayer. I have been deliberately searching for a spiritual father for most of a year. I don't know how to proceed."

"You *are* proceeding," he said.

"No, I mean I don't know where to find a spiritual guide, a father who will teach me, help me avoid pride and impatience and harsh thoughts."

"What do you do when you suffer pride, or impatience, or harsh thoughts toward other people?" he asked.

"Well, mostly I pray."

"Tell me how you pray."

"I say the Jesus Prayer."

"Do you say it slowly?" he asked.

"Well, I don't hurry."

"Do you listen to the words?"

"Yes."

"And to the stillness between the words?"

Hmm, I thought, then asked, "The stillness between the words?"

"When you pray the prayer, say it once, and then wait, listening. Then say it again. Then wait, listening."

"Yes, Father. I'll do that."

He stood up, saying, "I know you will."

As I knelt, he placed his stole over my head; then he took it away, and said, "Don't worry about the number of repetitions; just notice the words and the stillness."

"Yes, Father," I said, bowing my head, waiting for the prayers of absolution.

He stepped back. "You know," he said, "it is not you who prays."

"It's not," I repeated.

"No," he said. "This is why you must listen. You must learn that it is God who prays. When you descend into your heart, it is God you find, already praying in you."

Finally, he replaced the stole over my head, spoke the prayers of absolution, and blessed me, in the name "*tou Patrós kai tou Yióu kai tou Ágiou Pnévmatos.*"

I stood, kissed his hand, and said, "Thank you, Father. I think this will help. I'm eager to see if it does."

He blessed me again, and said, "Maybe you will come back and tell me how you are finding your way."

"A guide is good," he said, "but remember the Scriptures: 'When the Spirit of Truth comes, he will show you all things.' Don't wait for a guide. Pray."

Ben was waiting in a stall before Our Lady Esphagméni. He had his prayer rope in his hand, and looked up as I opened the door to leave the chapel.

"You took a while," he said. "Guess you had a lot to confess, huh?"

"Guess so. I had to confess my plans to beat my wise-guy son."

"Oooo," he said, "didn't the father tell you that might be unforgivable?"

———

We returned to the vigil to find every candle of every candelabra lit and all the huge fixtures circling in broad arcs, filling the nave with glittering golden light reflecting off a million golden surfaces. It was a feast of sparkling light, accompanied by celebratory festal chanting from two full choirs. To repeat the emissaries of old, "We didn't know if we were in heaven or on earth."

We stayed in that middle ground until a bit after 2:00 AM, when I happened to look over at Ben and saw that he was fighting to keep his eyes open. I nudged him, nodded toward the door, and led him out into the courtyard. We walked, blinking, into a glorious star-filled night. The air was cool and made me suddenly more fully awake.

"I'm feeling pretty wide awake now," I said, "Should we go back in?"

"Sure," Ben said, his eyes almost crossing as he spoke.

"Never mind," I said, and threw my arm around him to walk with him back to our room.

Ben slept for about three hours; I napped off and on, but was going over the words of Father Gregory, trying hard to remember all he'd said and to write it down as accurately as I could. His words resonated with me, and I knew that I had come across similar observations before. I'd read similar admonitions just days earlier in *The Authentic Seal*; still, they hadn't struck me then as they struck me now—as *possible*. More than that, they seemed, even, very likely. I was ready to pray slowly, and ready to attend to the stillness between prayers. I wanted to catch wind of the Holy Spirit praying in me.

That night, though, I didn't get very far. I woke with a start, prayer rope in hand, and looked at my watch; it was about 5:30 AM. The morning's Divine Liturgy would be a festal liturgy, and I didn't want Ben to miss the party. I grabbed his big toe and jiggled it to wake him. Good sport that he is, he jumped up and pulled on his clothes without a word of complaint. We scrambled over the stone courtyard, along the side of the trápeza, and arrived just as orthros was ending. We found stalls as the chanters intoned the doxology.

The icons—as well as the monks and pilgrims—were censed by a duo of deacons, moving from place to place in tandem, and bearing on their shoulders golden replicas of the katholikón. Ten priests—Father Gregory among them, I think—joined the presiding bishop of the feast for the processions and the readings, filling the air with celebratory, nearly raucous, full-throated chanting and filling the nave with their red and white vestments; again the candelabra was, as the liturgy proceeded, completely lit, filling the nave with wavering golden light. The iconostasis seemed to move with light. The nave and every narthex was lined with pilgrims and monks, celebrating the feast in prayer, witnessing anew the birth of the Church.

After nearly three hours of vertiginous beauty, we partook of the Holy Mysteries and of the festal bread soaked in honeyed wine. Following the final prayers, the bishop blessed us, giving us another square of antídoron as he did so, and the Church streamed into the bright morning to begin another year as the visible Body of Christ.

After a feast of roasted fish and potatoes, feta, olives, oranges, baklava, and a deep red wine, Ben and I collapsed in our room, where we napped for a few hours before meeting Father Matthew for our tour.

We had strolled the grounds on our own the day before, but Father Matthew augmented the walk with an array of stories. We toured the wine cellar, the rakí distillery, the several groves and gardens; he pointed out the various tilled fields, the workshops, the mill. At the end of our walk, he brought us to the cemetery chapel. We venerated the icons inside, then he led us around and below to the ossuary. It was empty.

"We decided it was time to clean it out, and restack the bones of our brothers," he said. "It's something we try to do every hundred years or so." He was smiling.

He pointed to an opening in the floor. "This time, we found another entire layer of bones in underground vaults. None of the living monks knew about them."

Ben and I just looked and listened.

"It was when the monks came down to organize the vaults in 1842 that they found Saint Evdókimos."

"Saint Evdókimos?" I asked.

He reached into his pocket and pulled out a small, laminated icon of the saint. He gave it to Ben. "The monks found the remains—the relics—of a monk seated far back behind the other bones. He was holding an icon of the Theotokos."

Father Matthew paused to let the story sink in.

"We didn't know his real name. All we knew is that when his time drew near, he told no one, but made his way down here cradling the icon, sat down in the very back, and fell asleep.

"When they found him, his bones were the color of golden beeswax, and the vault was filled with the fragrance of myrrh.

"We remember him now as Saint Evdókimos."

"Where are all the bones now?" I asked. "Where else can you keep a thousand years' worth of bones?"

He turned to the left and pointed. "Right there."

———

We had walked past a covered shed on our way in, but I was so intent on the chapel in front of me that I hadn't noticed what lay under the shed, protected from the elements by only a tin roof and a tarp.

"Come," he said, "meet my future roommates."

Father Matthew led us along a narrow plank between heaps of human bones. Along the right side of the plank, three other rows of planks reached a good thirty feet; along each of these, the skulls of more than a thousand monks had been carefully placed side by side. Some were gray, some white, some were very nearly black; a great many were the color of beeswax candles.

I felt a little dizzy.

Ben seemed fine, if fascinated, saying, "Whoa."

Father Matthew said, "Sort of makes a point, eh? All that we accomplish comes down pretty much to this."

The walk back to our room was fairly subdued. We left Father Matthew to prepare for Vespers, and Ben and I went to rest up a bit before the tálanton called us back to church.

———

To understand the unique character of the Vespers service of Pentecost Sunday—the Kneeling Vespers—it helps to have a sense of Pascha, our Easter Sunday. Following about fifty days—all told—of pre-Lenten and Lenten fasting, and more than a month of fairly demanding prayer services, Great Lent culminates in Holy Week, when the services become all the more demanding, but begin, incrementally, to replace the "bright sadness" of Lent and the Crucifixion with the giddy celebration of the Resurrection, observed in the midnight service of Holy Saturday night through the wee hours of Sunday morning. It's such a big deal for us—partaking in this movement from death to life—that we forgo kneeling altogether for the next fifty days.

The Vespers service following the Feast of Pentecost, then, is the service that reintroduces the practice of kneeling to the Church.

At Vatopédi, Ben and I had the added pleasure of kneeling with several hundred pilgrims and nearly a hundred monastic celebrants of a hierarchical Vespers. We returned to the practice of kneeling, then, in good company, and tasted again, if only slightly, the spirit of bright sadness of those who continue on the journey.

After trápeza, we relaxed by the monastery gate, where Ben spent the evening crumbling bits of bread for the huge carp in the reservoir there. I'd known he'd been pocketing bread from the trápeza, but didn't know until now that he was copping it for the carp. When he'd gone through his stash, we headed back to the room to turn in early.

I let Ben sleep through much of the midnight service, then grabbed his big toe in time for orthros. He'd been a very good sport, but I could see that he was exhausted; most nights, he'd fallen asleep as soon as he lay down.

We lit our candles in the exonarthex and venerated the icons on our way into the katholikón. We found places in the front row of chairs the monks had set up for pilgrims and enjoyed what would be our last Divine Liturgy, our final Communion, on the Holy Mountain.

———

We had hoped to spend one more night on Mount Athos; in particular, I hoped to introduce Ben to Father Zakarías at Xenofóndos. As it was, the Feast of Pentecost had brought hundreds of men to the Holy Mountain, and we weren't able to get tickets for the *Áxion Estín*— though, with about two hundred men clamoring for the last twenty tickets, we did get to enjoy a farewell shoving match.

The *Áxion Estín* would have made a regular stop at Xenofóndos, near the midpoint of its final run to Ouranoúpoli. As it turned out, we were able only to gain passage on the *Ágia Ánna*, which would, on its final northern run, make a beeline from Dáfni to Ouranoúpoli without any stops along the way.

So, we were a little disappointed, but as we looked ahead to two-plus hours with the crowd at Dáfni, we realized that if we boarded the *Ágia Ánna* early—if we hopped aboard now, as the boat prepared to pull out for its final *southward* run before heading north—we could finish our pilgrimage with what was essentially a boat tour taking us the entire length of the Holy Mountain.

When Ben and I had boarded the boat, we discovered that our friend Art Dimopoulos had come up with the same idea; we found him on the upper deck, visiting with friends from Koutloumousíou. After having forsaken stillness and calm in the turmoil of Karyés and Dáfni, we recovered a good bit of it as we cruised along the Athonite coast. At the far end, rounding the cliffs of Katounakía and turning back at Nimfé (the very tip of the peninsula), we raised our eyes to the cliffs where scattered, isolated dwellings perched high in chinks in the rock face. Here, the most strenuous ascetics had fashioned—out of the most exposed granite faces of the Holy Mountain—their solitary cave dwellings, enclosed by stone facades. We'd been staring up at them for a while when Art said, "I think I found that peace I lost in Karyés. If I lose it again, I will simply remember *this*."

——— Cave Dwellings of "the Desert" ———

Our final run north from the very "desert" of the Holy Mountain, to Ouranoúpoli, provided the visual aid for a final review of what had turned out to be a fruitful journey, even if it hadn't always—hadn't really *ever*—gone as expected. We passed beneath Saint Anna's Skete, where Fathers Seraphim and Theóphilos labored among their brothers; we rounded the next headland and passed along the slopes of New Skete, where the tomb of Elder Joseph the Hesychast sweetened a citrus grove; we passed Saint Paul's Monastery, where Yórgos, Stamátis, and their crew of accountants had welcomed me as one of their own, and we passed the sheer face of Dionysíou from which those same accountants had shouted their farewell to "Sakko" across the narrow valley; we passed the radiant enclave of Grigoríou, where Father Cosmás brightened the archondaríki with a ready smile and willing heart; and then we passed beneath the miraculous Simonópetra, where Ben and I had, I'd say, found our Athonite family and our Athonite home.

At Dáfni, the boat took on its final passengers, and we made for the mainland, passing before the enormity of Saint Panteleímon's Monastery, the generous Xenofóndos, where Father Zakarías, drawn as a young seminarian to a life of prayer, continued that journey. Our route took us past Docheiaríou—the first of the monasteries I'd seen, nine months earlier—and along the rugged and sparsely inhabited coast, where scattered hermitages and ancient ruins completed my passage just as it had begun.

16

Watch, therefore, and pray . . .

The journey to prayer, so far as I can tell, comes to no conclusive end. Like théosis itself, the pilgrim proceeds from glimpse to glimpse—or, as Saint Gregory of Nyssa speaks of the matter, *from glory to glory.* With the help of many along the way over the year, I felt as if, finally, I might have made a beginning.

Father Cosmás offered me his friendship, his willing counsel, and shared with me his own, ongoing struggle. He also gave me—simply by his willingness to hang out and talk, his willingness to laugh at me and at himself—a sustaining sense of joy. Even now, when I think of him, I see him smiling broadly, clapping his hands together, laughing, "*Doxa to Theo!*"

Father Gregory first helped me to confront the need to trust forgiveness. Then he helped me to attend to the stillness within and between the very words of prayer, and in so doing helped me to apprehend God's responsive presence, biding in the words that He is pleased to speak in us and through us.

Father Iákovos—and, through his book, Yéronda Aimilianós—opened for me the powerful sense that one must struggle, must insist, must strenuously cling to God. And Father Iákovos helped me to glimpse how this struggle is also something that God is pleased to assist, something that He has enabled in the first place.

I have also found a compelling witness—clear evidence of the sweetness of the journey—in the persons of Fathers Seraphim, Theóphilos, Matthew, Nicéphoros, George, Andrew, Iosíf, Damaskínos, and a host of others on the Holy Mountain and elsewhere. Just to see these men endeavoring to live the faith—giving their bodies, souls, and spirits to the performance of what their hearts and minds have seen fit to believe—provides powerful encouragement for the pilgrim who hopes within the scope of his own circumstance to do the same.

I hadn't found a father. I had found many.

And more than that, my conversations with those many living fathers, more often than not, reconnected me with a good many other fathers and mothers—living and asleep—whom I had met only on the written page, guides whose insights had been part of my journey already, but whose words I had not sufficiently opened.

Rather, theirs were insights that I had not yet been opened *by*.

The face-to-face meeting with these athletes of prayer awakened in me an experience of words I had read, but had not yet owned, had not yet performed, had not yet made flesh.

Even now, even as I write about this deep richness—this lush and available beauty that I am finally beginning to apprehend—I remain a little torn. I've come upon these treasures of the faith more or less piecemeal, bit by bit, along a slow and desultory path from Baptist kid to Presbyterian elder to Episcopal short-timer to being a parishioner in—as we say in the business—the "One Holy, Orthodox, Catholic, and Apostolic Church."

Even now, on occasion, I wonder if the better choice wouldn't have been to stay put. It certainly would have been the more aggravating choice, but I wonder if the braver choice would have been to remain in that besieged community where I was first taught the love of God, where I might have taken part in that community's recovery of a fullness that's been more or less *left behind*—as it were—by historical aberration and unfortunate, reactionary choices.

Water under the bridge, I suppose. If, where they sup, the soup seems thin to some, it will have to be up to them to recover the savor, to recover the banquet of our common inheritance.

———

This past July, Father Iákovos was ordained a priest; in time, I pray that he will also be recognized as the *pnevmatikós* I believe him to be, and that Ben might find in him the spiritual guide that I have sought for myself. In any event, I know that Ben and I will continue to seek his counsel, delight in his friendship.

I trust that in the near future, Marcia and Liz might join us for a pilgrimage to Ormylia and to the Monastery of the Annunciation there, where we might enjoy together our newly discovered extended family at Simonópetra.

———

The journey is endless, of course—intermittently difficult and intermittently easy as can be. However difficult it becomes, even the difficulty is sweetened by good companions along the way. Just as I've lived the better part—I should say the *worse* part—of my faith more or less in my head, I have lived many of those long years insufficiently accompanied. That is, I have not only squandered the embodied fullness of the faith; I have also squandered the life of the Body of Christ, the solace of lives together.

As for the pursuit of prayer?

So far. So good.

Prayer, in general, and the Jesus Prayer, in particular, have become the sustaining focus of my waking days, and they have become a surprising accompaniment to my nights. I sleep less, waking every few hours—sometimes more often—to find the prayer on my lips. I spend a good bit of each night walking through the dark house, standing before the wavering vigil light of our family altar and icon wall, remembering friends and family—the living and the dead—in prayer. The more I do this, the more I want to do this.

As for a *life of prayer*? I'd say I'm finally heading that way, though I haven't yet arrived—far from it.

Still, I can say that I have tasted it.

Just now, I can almost see it.

EPILOGUE

The phone call came in the middle of my last poetry class of the spring semester. I had switched off the ringer for class, but the phone kept humming in my pocket for a while before it stopped. I went on with my last bit of yammering at my students, wishing them all a good and productive summer before sending them on their way.

As soon as the room cleared, I pulled out my cell phone to see who had called. I didn't recognize the number, but hit the *call back* button anyway.

The voice at the other end said simply, "Christ is Risen."

"Truly He is Risen," I replied. "Who is this?"

I heard a chuckle, and a laughing reply, "*Who is this, you ask?*" I recognized the chuckle, as well as the laughing voice.

"Father Iákovos?" I asked.

"*Yes*, Father Iákovos. How are you, Isaák?"

"*Doxa to Theo*," I said. "We're all well, and savoring Bright Week hereabouts. And you, Father? You're well?"

"*Doxa to Theo*."

———

I had seen Father Iákovos during the previous December, when my son Ben and I had made a brief visit to Simonópetra, the monastery that has become our Athonite home. It was Ben's third trip, and my eighteenth—hard as that is to believe. At that time, Father Iákovos had informed us that he would be coming to America for a year beginning, perhaps, in February.

All the monks of Mount Athos receive their assignments for the following year—their *diakonía*—during these winter months, assignments that lead them either to new duties or to continued labor at their current assignments. Over the years, Father Iákovos's *diakonía* have been fairly varied, including his serving the monastery as tailor, dentist, guestmaster, chanter, and priest. At the request of Abbot Eliséos, Father Iákovos became a priest-monk in 2006. Soon thereafter, he became a confessor, a *pnevmatikós*, as well. The news that he would be in the States for an extended period was very good news indeed. Something about his unshakeable joy always lifts my spirit whenever our paths cross, and I was hoping that his time in America would avail a good number of path-crossings, and closer to home.

———

I have been blessed to have seen my pilgrimages to the Holy Mountain become a nearly annual (sometimes twice-annual) occasion. Over the years, I have learned to narrow the reach of my wandering somewhat, to allow more time with beloved fathers at Simonópetra, Vatopédi, Xenofóndos, and Grigoríou; that is to say, I have been able to travel more deeply into these communities, if less broadly among them.

Eight years ago, I established a study-abroad program in Greece, a writing-focused workshop that has enabled frequent visits to my adopted country. That program itself has morphed into an independent enterprise, "Writing Workshops in Greece, LLC," which brings young and established writers—poets, fiction writers, playwrights, memoirists, essayists, food and travel writers, and so on—together for two- or four-week sessions in writers' paradise. Over the years, it has become my pleasure during these workshop sessions to introduce a few willing pilgrims at a time to my beloved Holy Mountain. We generally go for a long weekend to Vatopédi, where Father Matthew arranges our entry, and graciously presents what I like to call a short course in Orthodox Monasticism 101. My fellow travelers have been pretty various—students young and old, a few fellow faculty, Catholics, Protestants, agnostics, and skeptics—but each has come away amazed at the undeniable beauty and spiritual radiance of these enclaves, of their monks, and of their lives of prayer. What began—to be honest— as a fairly selfish excuse to make the Holy Mountain a continuing part of my life has become a delightful opportunity to share this treasure with a willing few.

So, over the past dozen years, this practice of pilgrimage has enriched my journey and—I pray it is so—has enriched the journeys of a good many others. This practice of pilgrimage has, moreover, allowed me to glimpse the profound degree to which the notion of *pilgrimage* turns out to be a very likely figure for life itself—the journey that is not so much a matter of hurrying to a destination as it is a matter of attending to the road before us, and attending to the fragile surround—those persons, places, and countless things that accompany us as we proceed.

Every time I set foot again on the Holy Mountain I am immediately overcome with a sense of homecoming—as if I am once more at the threshold of returning to myself, recovering again a renewed sense of myself as a member of Christ's Body. Life in *the world*, as it were, is difficult and distracting; I have come to depend upon these homecomings as a regular renewal, a recharging, a corrective reorientation. As a result, every time I board the boat to return back to *the world*, it is with a measure of recovered purpose, renewed strength.

The experience, in general, brings to mind what Robert Frost observes in "Birches."

It's when I'm weary of considerations,
And life is too much like a pathless wood
Where your face burns and tickles with the cobwebs
Broken across it, and one eye is weeping
From a twig's having lashed across it open.
I'd like to get away from earth awhile
And then come back to it and begin over.

So yes, that's what these retreats to the Holy Mountain have come to mean to me; and yes, these journeys are "good both going and coming back."

All of this is to say that, *sigá, sigá* (slowly, slowly), my continued relationship with the Athonite fathers and with their prayer tradition has enabled me to apprehend, albeit obliquely, how it is we pass from death to life, how the mortal human person is made immortal—without forsaking humanness.

May it be blessed.

Short Trip to the Edge

*And then I was standing at the edge. It would surprise you
how near to home. And the abyss? Every shade of blue,
all of them readily confused, and, oddly, none of this
as terrifying as I had expected, just endless.*

*What? You find this business easy? When every breath is thick
with heady vapor from the edge? You might not be so quick
to deny what prefers its more dramatic churning done
out of sight. Enough about you. The enormity spun,*

*and I spun too, and reached across what must have been its dome.
When I was good and dizzy (since it was so near), I went home.*

ACKNOWLEDGMENTS

With gratitude to the University of Missouri Research Council, whose research leave afforded me time to travel and to write.

With love to Marcia, Elizabeth, and Benjamin, whose patience and sacrifice allowed me to commence a long-desired journey.

With gratitude to Nikolaos Sanidas, publisher of Parrisia Editions of Athens, Greece, whose kindness resulted in the Greek edition of this book, Μικρό Ταξίδι στη Μεθόριο, 2014, and also in the photographs from that edition being made available for this English edition.

I also extend warm thanks to Polyxeni Tsaliki, Ioanna P. Koutri, and Thanos V. Kiosoglou for their translation efforts on the Greek edition.

"Setting Out" first appeared in *Compass of Affection: Poems New & Selected*, published by Paraclete Press in 2006.

"Regarding the Body" and "Short Trip to the Edge" appeared in *Recovered Body*, reprinted by Eighth Day Press in 2003.

The quotation from Robert Frost's poem "Birches" is from *The Poetry of Robert Frost: The Collected Poems, Complete and Unabridged* (New York: Holt, Rinehart and Winston, 1979), 121–22.

Antídoron This is the blessed bread from which a particular portion ("the Lamb") is removed and consecrated for the Eucharist. The remnant is then cut into small squares and offered to all present. The word means "instead of the gifts," indicating that it may be received even by those who do not partake of the Eucharist.

Archondaríki Archondaríki is probably the first Greek word a pilgrim learns. It is the reception area of a monastic enclave; upon arrival, the pilgrim is expected to stop here, where he will sign in, perhaps have his *diamonitírion* inspected, and, if he's staying the night, be assigned a room. This is most often accompanied by some degree of welcome and refreshment; it is sometimes accompanied by what feels more like interrogation.

Arsanás The water port of a monastic enclave, the *arsánas* is the primary point of entry for those monasteries and *sketes* along the coast. Each of the twenty monasteries, even those located some miles inland, maintains an *arsánas* on their lands for sending and receiving goods and for periodic travel.

Ascesis The athletic effort—in terms of prayer, fasting, prostrations, all-night vigils, and so on—of subduing the passions, *ascesis* focuses the distracted mind, unifying the scattered *nous*, assisting the practitioner toward *hesychía*, which is an acquired stillness, a spiritual calm, understood to be a partaking of the kingdom of God even now.

Coenobitic Communities in which a common rule is observed by all the brotherhood—as well as common worship and common meals—are called *coenobitic*. All twenty of the ruling monasteries on Mount Athos have returned to a coenobitic rule. See *idiorrhythmic* below.

Diamonitírion This is the official document that allows entry to the Holy Mountain. It indicates the dates of an initial, four-day visit, which may be extended at the Pilgrims' Bureau office in Karyés. It also indicates one's religion.

Dikaíos   The "abbot" of a *skete*, the *dikaíos* is elected annually by the brotherhood.

Eremite   The term from which the word "hermit" derives, the *eremite* (or solitary) is a monk who lives alone, pursuing an extreme form of *ascesis*. Such are the cave dwellers of the Athonite wilderness, many of whom live in the areas called Vígla and Katanoukía at the southern tip of the Holy Mountain.

Hegúmenos   The "abbot" of a monastery, the *hegúmenos* is often its spiritual father as well, though one or more other, respected elders may also serve as spiritual father for monks and for pilgrims. The *hegúmenos* of a monastery is elected for life.

Hesychía   The condition that the *hesychast* struggles to attain, *hesychía* is an apprehension of stillness, calm, and a partaking of the presence of God.

Hesychast   The *hesychast* is the man or woman who pursues *hesychía*, that stillness availing experiential knowledge of God's presence.

Iconostásis   This is the icon wall spanning the width of the sanctuary and protecting from view the holy altar and, to its left, the table of oblation where the Communion elements are prepared for consecration. The wall has a double door in its center—the Royal Doors—through which only the priest will pass, and two single doors—Deacons' Doors—at the far left and right ends of the wall. The icon of Christ is always immediately to the right of the Royal Doors, and the icon of the Theotokos is always immediately to the left. The icon of Saint John the Baptist is generally placed to the right of Christ, and the name-saint of the church or chapel is generally placed to the left of the Theotokos. The Archangels Michael and Gabriel are either on or near the Deacons' Doors, with Gabriel generally on the left and Michael generally on the right.

Idiorrhythmic These are communities in which monks are allowed, under direction of a spiritual father, to pursue individual—often very strenuous— rules of prayer and *ascesis*. On the Holy Mountain, certain of the *sketes* and certain smaller enclaves observe an *idiorrhythmic* rule.

The Jesus Prayer The "long form" of this very short and very revealing prayer is "Lord Jesus Christ, Son of God, have mercy on me, a sinner." It is also called "the Prayer of the Heart," "Noetic Prayer," and has been called "the Prayer of the Holy Mountain." The practice of this prayer is what led me, over the course of many years, to Orthodoxy, and thereafter to a hunger for a life of prayer.

Katholikón The main church of a monastery, the *katholikón* is usually located at the center of the enclave that is protected by the monastery's original, walled structure.

Kyriakón This is the main church of a *skete*, a monastic enclave that is not formally understood, on the Holy Mountain, as one of the twenty ruling monasteries.

Kéllia The cells of the monks, one's *kéllia* can be either a room in a monastery or a separate structure. The *kéllia* of an *eremite* can be as simple as a cave in the face of a cliff.

Monopathi These are the footpaths that connect one community to another. Some are well used and well maintained, but many are overgrown. Until relatively recently, walking these paths was the only way to move inland among the monasteries; for many monks and for most pilgrims, the microbuses have become the primary mode of overland travel.

Mystérion In the Eastern Church, *mystérion* is the preferred term for *sacrament* in general. Most specifically, *mystérion* refers to the Eucharist.

Komboskíni Also called a *chótki* by Slavonic Orthodox, the *komboskíni* is the prayer rope, usually a knotted, black wool cord or a string of wooden beads, used by those who practice the prayer of the heart, which is, most often, some version of the *Jesus Prayer*.

Komboloi These are the popular "worry beads" that provide a rhythmic clack to accompany almost any café scene. Sort of a secular version of *komboskíni*, the *komboloi* are more likely to accompany a game of dominoes or backgammon than contemplative prayer.

Nous Variously—and never adequately—translated, the *nous* is the faculty of the human person that apprehends God's presence and intuits God's will; it can become, when purified, God's agency acting within the human heart. A clouded *nous*, a distracted *nous*, a fragmented *nous* (afflictions that most of us suffer), are responsible for imbalances of perception, wherein a person may become unduly enamored of flesh, or unduly disrespecting of the body, or unduly attached to created things rather than to their Creator. A purified *nous* allows one to see and to honor God, who is All in all.

Panagía Another common name for the Virgin Mary, *Panagía* (All Holy) foregrounds her knowing acquiescence to the will of God, her example as one who chose to cooperate with the Holy Word.

Phiále This is the large font—usually covered by a domed, and icon-laden pergola—where the service of the blessing of the waters takes place. In parishes, this blessing happens once or twice during the Feast of Theophany; here on the Holy Mountain, the blessing of the waters is generally a monthly event.

Pilgrim Hardly ever—these days—a musket-packing Puritan with buckles on his boots, a *pilgrim* is a person who, confronted by a spiritual distance to be crossed, determines to undertake that journey.

Pnevmatikós
A "spirit-bearer" and confessor, he is an elder whose gifts include insight into the spiritual well-being of his spiritual children. In a monastery setting, the *pnevmatikós* is trusted to hear confession, and to give related counsel for avoiding recurrent sin.

Sémantron This is a wooden board (chestnut being a popular choice) occurring in lengths ranging from five to eight feet (give or take) that is most often carved to accommodate a handgrip in its center. Each end is also carved to affect something of an *o*-shape, with a hole bored into the center of each *o* for the purpose of resonance. The *sémantron* is struck rhythmically with a mallet to indicate an approaching time of common worship.

Skete (*skiti*) A (usually) smaller community of brothers, and a dependency of one of the ruling monasteries. While all Athonite monasteries are now *coenobitic*, many of the sketes remain *idiorrhythmic*.

Tálanton This curved metal version of the *sémantron* (often in the shape of an omega) is also called a *bílo* among Russian and other Slavonic traditions. For the sake of (perhaps) efficacious confusion, the terms *sémantron* and *tálanton* are used interchangeably in some monasteries.

Theotokos Theotokos is a name for the Virgin Mary that foregrounds her being "God-bearer," the Mother of God, the paradox of which is deliberate and, one hopes, illuminating.

Trápeza This is the "refectory," usually a large, open hall whose walls—and, in some cases, ceilings—are covered with icon murals. These dining halls are furnished with long tables and benches, with a smaller table in a place of honor, where sits the abbot and those who directly assist in his ministry and administration, as well as, occasionally, certain honored guests. The hall nearly always includes a lectern—sometimes a raised pulpit fixed into a wall and mounted by a small staircase—from which a reader provides excerpts from Scripture or the lives of the saints.

Vládika In Slavonic churches, a bishop or abbot is addressed as *Vládika*, which is to say "Master."

Yéronda Literally "old one," *yéronda* is a term of respect. The abbot or *diakaíos* of a monastery or *skete*, or an "elder," a spiritual father will be addressed this way. It is not uncommon for any elderly monk to be addressed as *yéronda*, as a gesture of loving respect.

ABOUT PARACLETE PRESS

Who We Are

Paraclete Press is a publisher of books, recordings, and DVDs on Christian spirituality. Our publishing represents a full expression of Christian belief and practice—from Catholic to Evangelical, from Protestant to Orthodox. We are the publishing arm of the Community of Jesus, an ecumenical monastic community in the Benedictine tradition. As such, we are uniquely positioned in the marketplace without connection to a large corporation and with informal relationships to many branches and denominations of faith.

What We Are Doing

Paraclete Press Books | Paraclete publishes books that show the richness and depth of what it means to be Christian. Although Benedictine spirituality is at the heart of all that we do, we publish books that reflect the Christian experience across many cultures, time periods, and houses of worship. We publish books that nourish the vibrant life of the church and its people.

We have several different series, including the best-selling Paraclete Essentials and Paraclete Giants series of classic texts in contemporary English; Voices from the Monastery—men and women monastics writing about living a spiritual life today; award-winning poetry; best-selling gift books for children on the occasions of baptism and first communion; and the Active Prayer Series that brings creativity and liveliness to any life of prayer.

Mount Tabor Books | Paraclete's newest series, Mount Tabor Books, focuses on the arts and literature as well as liturgical worship and spirituality, and was created in conjunction with the Mount Tabor Ecumenical Centre for Art and Spirituality in Barga, Italy.

Paraclete Recordings | From Gregorian chant to contemporary American choral works, our recordings celebrate the best of sacred choral music composed through the centuries that create a space for heaven and earth to intersect. Paraclete Recordings is the record label representing the internationally acclaimed choir Gloriæ Dei Cantores, praised for their "rapt and fathomless spiritual intensity" by *American Record Guide*; the Gloriæ Dei Cantores Schola, specializing in the study and performance of Gregorian chant; and the other instrumental artists of the Gloriæ Dei Artes Foundation.

Paraclete Press is also privileged to be the exclusive North American distributor of the recordings of the Monastic Choir of St. Peter's Abbey in Solesmes, France, long considered to be a leading authority on Gregorian chant.

Paraclete Videos | Our DVDs offer spiritual help, healing, and biblical guidance for a broad range of life issues including grief and loss, marriage, forgiveness, facing death, bullying, addictions, Alzheimer's, and spiritual formation.

Learn more about us at our website:
www.paracletepress.com or
phone us toll-free at 1.800.451.5006

SCAN
TO
READ
MORE

Slow Pilgrim
The Collected Poems of Scott Cairns
Scott Cairns

ISBN: 978-1-61261-657-5, $39.00, French flap paperback

"Among American poets of religious belief at the present time, none is more skillful, authentic, or convincing than Scott Cairns."
—B. H. Fairchild, poet, National Book Critics Circle Award winner

99 Psalms
Said
Translated by Mark S. Burrows

ISBN: 978-1-61261-294-2, $17.99, Paperback

These are poems of praise and lament, of questioning and wondering. In the tradition of the Hebrew psalmist, they find their voice in exile, in this case one that is both existential and geographical.

Eyes Have I That See
John Julian

ISBN: 978-1-61261-640-7, $18.00, Paperback

From rough folk-verse to high-flown poesy, from a nine-line rhyme to a six-hundred-line epic, both the style and genre of the poetry in this volume cover a broad range of poetic possibility. This is the first volume of John Julian's poetry ever published, revealing an important new American poetic voice.

Available from most booksellers or through Paraclete Press:
www.paracletepress.com | 1-800-451-5006
Try your local bookstore first.